Sweet
NOSHINGS

Sweet Noshings

NEW TWISTS ON TRADITIONAL JEWISH DESSERTS

AMY KRITZER,

Founder of

ROCK
POINT
QUARTOKNOWS.COM
NEW YORK, NY

Quarto is the authority on a wide range of topics.

Quarto educates, entertains and enriches the lives of our readers—enthusiasts and lovers of hands-on living.

www.quartoknows.com

Text and Photography © 2016 Amy Kritzer

First published in the United States of America in 2016 by
Rock Point, a member of
Quarto Publishing Group USA Inc.
142 West 36th Street, 4th Floor
New York, NY 10018

quartoknows.com

10 9 8 7 6 5 4 3 2

ISBN: 978-1-63106-179-0

Food photography by Amy Kritzer
Photograph on page 49 and back cover © Colin Cooke (Peanut Butter and Dark Chocolate Babka)
Author Photographs by Tim Kyle
Author Photograph on page 13 by Juliet Mullins
Interior design by Marc J. Cohen

Printed in China

To *Andypooh,* who loves cookies.

And to *Bubbe,* who is already bragging

to her friends at the JCC.

Contents

Cookies

Cakes and Breads

Flourless (Pesach) Desserts

Latkes, Egg Creams, Kugel, and More!

Introduction

I almost started an all-cupcake blog.
Aren't Jew glad I didn't?

It was late November, close enough to Thanksgiving that most of our clients were out of the office. But far enough away that I still had to sit at my desk and pretend I had work to do. I started browsing cooking blogs, as I often did after exhausting Facebook, but this time I had a different purpose. I was thinking of starting my own. It would be a fun hobby, and a little break from my current cubicle-monkey existence.

Initially, my mind went to desserts. I love a good celebration, and cupcakes say "I'm here to paaar-taaay." Plus, is there anything better than baking a treat for someone and seeing them nearly pass out from enjoyment?

Then I talked to my brother Andrew about it. He was, and is, my go-to source for business questions. He wondered if I would want to bake cupcakes every week. Forever. And maybe they were just a bit trendy? He had a point.

He was the one who suggested Jewish food. (I won't take the credit for the idea, but the name "What Jew Wanna Eat" was all mine!) I loved the concept immediately. Jews and food just go together. You can hardly have one without the other. As a child, I thought of bagels, blintzes, and rugelach as just food, not Jewish food. And they were such an integral part of growing up Jewish. I thought of sweet and tangy brisket at Rosh Hashanah, whitefish salad at a bris, Manischewitz at a bar mitzvah, and blintzes at Shavuot. Where there are Jews, there's food. And kvetching. And worrying. But mostly food.

It's amazing how a smell or taste can bring you back to a specific place. I have a very distinct memory of making rugelach with my Bubbe in her sunshine-yellow floral wallpapered kitchen: rolling out circles of dough, sprinkling the cinnamon-sugar filling, and rolling the croissant-like cookies while sneaking a few nibbles of raw dough. (She would shoo me away just before it was time to clean up.) It was a recipe my Bubbe learned from her Bubbe, which made it extra-special.

I made my very first post on *What Jew Wanna Eat* for Hanukkah in 2010. Latkes immediately came to mind, but I wanted to put my own spin on things. Sweet potato latkes! And cinnamon applesauce. While it wasn't my most creative recipe, it was a start, and I was hooked. That idea—of taking traditional recipes and modernizing them with current ingredients and techniques—became my signature. I like paying homage to the classics, making them fun—and then feeding them to willing friends and boyfriends (much to their delight). Because isn't that what cooking is all about?

After a few months of blogging, I was totally in love. I had already made a few amazing Internet friends, and I counted the minutes until I could get back in the kitchen. I knew cubicleville was no longer for me, so I quit my job and attended culinary school, did supermarket demos (look out, Rachael Ray!), taught cooking classes, and even sold Jell-O shots at a piano bar. I had never been happier—and I've never looked back.

But let's back up a second. What the heck is Jewish food anyway? I once posed this question on my *WJWE* Facebook page. The answers ranged from kosher food to bagels and lox and even Chinese food. (If you've ever been to a Chinese restaurant on Christmas Eve, you get it.) Responses also included foods like knishes and shakshuka. Jewish food represents our history as a people; it connects us to our past and our future. But just as Jews have adapted and evolved with each new place we call home, so should our food. Even if that means covering macaroons with rainbow sprinkles. Mmm, sprinkles.

There is something comforting in traditions, for example, kneading challah dough just as our relatives once did. It's almost as if your Bubbe is right there in the kitchen with you. But there is also something powerful about taking those traditions, and making them our own—making new classics with flavors that incite memories but taste current.

Living in Texas, I like to incorporate local spices. If you look at the history of Jewish food (I highly recommend Gil Marks's tome *The Encyclopedia of Jewish Food*), you'll see Jewish food has always evolved. Some of the foods we know and love today were hardly around a hundred years ago, let alone thousands. Who says they can't continue to grow with new flavors and techniques?

We have access to more ingredients than ever before: exotic spices, fruits, grains. This isn't the land of potatoes and beets our ancestors had. There is no reason you can't throw a little cayenne into chocolate rugelach or a splash or ten of whiskey into a honey cake.

And then, of course, there is kosher. Does Jewish food have to be kosher? That's a debate for a whole other day. And while everything in this book is kosher (bacon in dessert is just plain wrong any way you look at it), I do use a lot of dairy. Because let's face it: Butter and cream taste good. And I'd rather eat a fruit salad than go near margarine myself. I offer substitutions whenever possible, so I hope everyone can enjoy these recipes!

When I started my blog, I thought I was writing just about food, and I thought only my Bubbe was reading. But then I started getting emails. There was the girl who lost her mother at a young age and never had her recipes; she was making mine to connect with her history. And there was the newlywed who married into a Jewish family and now makes my kugel in an attempt to impress the in-laws (it's working). As I read their stories, often through tears, I soon realized this was about way more than just food.

This book isn't just for Jews either. It's for people who love food, culture, history, sugar, and rainbow sprinkles. For people who aren't afraid of a little—or a lot—of butter. Not all of these recipes are quick and easy. Yeasted sweets and breads take time, and sometimes deep-frying is scary—albeit delicious—but I promise the time you spend connecting with these traditional recipes with a twist will be worth the effort. I focused on the Ashkenazi desserts I grew up with, with some Sephardic and other Jewish recipes thrown in. It's by no means exhaustive of all Jewish desserts, but it includes my new and old favorites. I hope you'll find a new favorite as well.

Mazel,

Amy

What Does Kosher Mean?

The word kosher comes from the word for "fit" in Hebrew and is a set of food dos and don'ts first recorded in the Hebrew Bible. The basic rules are no pork, no shellfish, and no mixing milk and meat products. So a bacon cheeseburger is definitely out. Today, not all Jews follow these laws about what animals to eat, how they should be slaughtered and prepared, and which foods may be eaten together. Some follow some kosher laws, such as not eating pork, while others are strictly observant. For many, keeping kosher is a constant reminder of their Jewish identity. Traditional Jewish foods like knishes, bagels, blintzes, and matzah ball soup can all be non-kosher if not prepared in accordance with Jewish law. Likewise, food can be kosher but not culturally Jewish. This book pays homage to traditional Jewish sweets and many recipes have dairy. But you can replace most with non-dairy milk and margarine to make them "parve" (containing neither dairy nor meat). Ess gezunterhait!

Amy with Bubbe

Helpful Tools

Pots and Pans

Two 9 x 5-in (23 x 13 cm) loaf pans
2 twelve-cup muffin pans
One to Three 12 x 8-in (30 x 20 cm) pans
12-cup (2.8 L) Bundt pan
Springform pan
9 x 13-in (23 x 33 cm) ceramic or glass pan
Baking sheets
Nonstick 9-in (23 cm) sauté pan
Sauce and sauté pans
Stockpot
Heavy-bottomed pot
Roasting pan

Kitchen Tools

Spatulas
Measuring cups and spoons (2 sets)
Prep bowls
Mixing bowls
Mixing spoons
Rolling pin
Strainers (large and small)
Deep-frying thermometer
Food thermometer
Measuring tape/ruler
Paring knife
Dough scraper
Pastry brush
3-in (7.5 cm) round cookie cutter
Cooling racks
Whisks (large and small)
Serrated knife

Small Appliances

Food processor
Stand mixer
Hand mixer
Ice cream maker

Pantry Staples

Aluminum foil
Parchment paper
Plastic wrap

Helpful Tips

Double boiler

You don't need to purchase a special double boiler; just make one at home. Double boilers are helpful for when you don't want ingredients on direct heat as they may burn, such as curds, meringues, or melting chocolate. To make one, simmer a few inches of water in a saucepan. Place a glass or metal bowl on top (or another saucepan) that fits tight. Make sure the water does not touch the bottom of the bowl.

Yeast

Don't fear the yeast! I mix dry yeast with a little sugar and warm water/milk (use a thermometer to make sure it's 110°F/43°C). The sugar helps activate the yeast. After 10 minutes, the yeast should be very foamy. If not, either the yeast is dead or the water was too cool to activate or too hot and you killed it. Try again with fresh yeast. This step is crucial to yeast success! When your dough is rising, place it in a warm but not too hot spot. I like to place mine on top of a warm (200°F/93°C) oven, on my dryer, or outside on a hot Texas day (okay, I just did this once but it worked!).

Rotating pans

For even baking, I rotate 2 cookie pans by turning them around and swapping spots in the oven halfway through the baking time.

Cookies

I think I was born to be a Texan. I love big hair, country music, and cowboys (and their trucks). But as one ex-boyfriend (who believes Texas should be its own country and that chicken fried steak is a food group) told me, I'll never be a Texan. Unlike places like my former home of NYC, where tenure gives you legitimacy as a resident, if you aren't born in Texas, you'll never be a Texan. But that doesn't stop me from incorporating Austin flavors into my Jewish recipes. Whether it's a cayenne kick and local pecans in Chocolate Rugelach, jalapeños in my potato latkes, or just some "Keep Austin Weird" flair in my Ombré Layer Cookies, I may never be a Texan, but I certainly can nosh like one.

Baklava-Spiced Rugelach

Prep time: 1 hour · Inactive prep time: overnight · Cook time: 50 minutes (25 minutes per batch) · Makes: 48 cookies

Rugelach, the Ashkenazi flaky cookie filled with awesomeness (yes, that's the technical definition), are traditionally filled with cinnamon and nuts or chocolate. I took the nut version up a notch with candied ginger (to add some spice) and cardamom (one of the main spices in chai tea). Inspired by baklava, I chose pistachios and almonds for the nut filling. Use this basic dough as a great base for any filling—jams, nuts, Nutella. I won't stop you!

For dough

½ cup (100 g) granulated sugar

3 teaspoons cardamom

⅛ teaspoon kosher salt

2 cups (284 g) all-purpose flour, plus more for rolling out dough

2 sticks or 1 cup (225 g) cold unsalted butter, cut into chunks

8 ounces (227 g) cold cream cheese, cut into chunks

⅓ cup sour cream

2 teaspoons vanilla extract

For filling

1 cup (125 g) slivered almonds (whole almonds, that works too)

1 cup (150 g) unsalted shelled pistachios (or additional almonds)

¼ cup (40g) candied ginger

¼ cup (50g) granulated sugar, plus more for sprinkling

¼ cup (60 ml) honey

1 ground teaspoon cardamom

1 ground teaspoon cinnamon

¼ teaspoon kosher salt (omit if using salted nuts)

½ stick or ¼ cup (55 g) unsalted butter, melted and cooled

1 egg

1 tablespoon water

1. Let's make the dough. In a medium bowl, whisk together sugar, cardamom, salt, and flour. Place flour mixture, butter, and cream cheese in a large food processor and pulse just until combined. You should have a fine, pea-size crumbly dough. Then add sour cream and vanilla. Pulse just until incorporated; do not over mix. Dough will still be a little crumbly.

2. If you don't have a food processor, let butter and cream cheese come to room temperature. With a stand or hand mixer with paddle attachment, cream together butter, cream cheese, and sugar just until light and fluffy, about 2 minutes. Then add sour cream, vanilla, and salt and combine. Lastly, add flour and cardamom and mix until just combined.

3. Remove dough from the food processor, removing the blade first, and form into a ball on a clean lightly floured surface, handling as little as possible.

4. Divide the dough into 4 balls (use a scale to make them equal) and flatten into disks, without working the dough too much. Dough will be slightly sticky. Wrap each in plastic wrap and chill overnight. The dough also freezes well for up to 2 months.

5. To make filling, pulse almonds, pistachios, and ginger in a food processor until broken down into tiny chunks, being careful not to form a paste. Then add sugar, honey, cardamom, cinnamon, salt, and melted butter and pulse to combine. You should have a sticky but crumbly filling.

6. When ready to bake, set 2 racks in the middle of the oven, and preheat to 350°F/180°C.

7. In a small bowl, whisk egg with water and set aside.

8. One at a time, keeping the other dough disks refrigerated, roll each dough disk on a lightly floured surface with a floured rolling pin into a 9-inch (23 cm) circle, ⅛-inch (3 mm) thick. To make a perfectly round circle, you can use a large bowl or cake pan turned upside down. Try to work fast as the dough is harder to manage as it warms up. Make sure to use enough flour on both sides to prevent sticking, but not so much that the dough gets dry. I like to flip the circle partway through rolling and re-flour the surface.

9. Sprinkle about one quarter of the filling onto the circle, leaving a ¼-inch (6 mm) border along the edge of the circle, and gently press into dough.

10. Cut the circle into 12 triangles like you would a pizza. The easiest way to do this is to cut the dough into quarters, and then cut each quarter into 3 pieces. (You can use a ruler if you want to be super-precise!) Roll each triangle from the wide end to the point, and secure the tip into the cookie so you have a little spiral. Place cookies on a parchment paper–lined baking sheet, 1 inch (2.5 cm) apart, with the dough point down. Repeat with remaining dough. Freeze for 30 minutes to prevent spreading. Wash the rugelach with egg mixture and sprinkle with more granulated sugar or coarse sugar if you prefer.

11. Bake for 20–25 minutes or until golden brown, switching sheet positions and rotating halfway through baking. Cool for 5 minutes on the baking sheet, and then remove and cool completely on cooling racks. Repeat with remaining cookies.

Tip

Cardamom can be expensive, so I buy it in the bulk spice aisle and keep it for a long time.

Tex-Mex Chocolate Rugelach

Prep time: 1 hour • Inactive prep time: 2 hours • Cook time: 25 minutes • Makes: about 28 cookies

I think I was born to be a Texan. I love big hair, country music, and cowboys (and their boots). This inspired me to put a little spice—and local pecans—into my rugelach. This version uses yeast to make a croissant-rugelach hybrid.

For dough

2¼ teaspoons (1 packet) active
   dry yeast
½ cup (120 ml) warm milk (110°F/43°C)
¼ cup (50 g) plus 1 teaspoon
   granulated sugar
3–4 cups (426–568 g) all-purpose flour
1 egg
2 sticks or 1 cup (225 g) unsalted
   butter, melted and cooled
1 teaspoon vanilla extract
¼ teaspoon kosher salt

For filling

6 tablespoons (85 g) unsalted butter,
   melted and cooled
8 ounces (230 g) semisweet or milk
   chocolate, chopped
1 cup (200 g) granulated sugar
¼ teaspoon kosher salt
¼ cup (22 g) unsweetened cocoa
   powder
Pinch cayenne pepper (or to taste,
   depending on how spicy you like it!)
2 teaspoons ground cinnamon
½ teaspoon nutmeg

For glaze

1/3 cup (80 ml) water
2/3 cup (133 g) granulated sugar

1. Let's make dough. In a large stand mixer bowl, whisk together yeast, milk, and 1 teaspoon sugar until the yeast dissolves. Let stand for 10 minutes until yeast gets foamy and puffs up. If your yeast does not get foamy, start over. Either your yeast is old, or the milk was too warm or too cool.

2. Add remaining sugar and 3 cups (426 g) flour and mix on medium speed with a dough hook until combined. Add in egg, butter, vanilla, and salt and mix for 5–7 minutes, until you have a smooth, slightly sticky dough. Add more flour if the dough is sticking to the bowl.

3. Place dough in a lightly greased bowl, cover, and let rise in a warm place (on top of an oven set to 200°F/93°C works great) for 1–2 hours, until doubled in size. At this point, you can use the dough right away or refrigerate for up to 2 days. The dough will just get better!

4. Next, make filling. In a small saucepan, melt butter over medium-low heat, and stir in chocolate to melt; remove from heat and stir in sugar, salt, cocoa powder, cayenne, cinnamon, and nutmeg.

5. Line 2 baking sheets with parchment paper.

6. Divide the dough in 2 pieces, keeping the part you aren't using covered. With a rolling pin on a clean surface, roll out the dough into a 6 x 21-inch (15 x 53 cm) rectangle. Measure about 3 inches (7.5 cm) across the bottom of a long side, and cut a triangle from the base to the top. Repeat to make triangles across the whole rectangle, alternating the base from bottom to top and making about 14 triangles. Flatten each triangle with your hand as much as you can and spread a thin layer of chocolate mixture on each one. I use my fingers for this part. Sprinkle with pecans, if desired. Then, starting at the wide end, roll triangles into croissants, careful to keep the filling intact.

7. Place the rugelach on the baking sheet, about 1 inch (2.5 cm) apart, with the tip on the bottom. Repeat with the remaining dough. Refrigerate for 30 minutes.

8. Preheat oven to 325°F/170°C with 2 racks in the center of the oven. Bake for 20–25 minutes or until golden brown, rotating the pans halfway through baking.

9. While rugelach are baking, make glaze. In a small saucepan, bring water and sugar to a boil, and simmer for 5 minutes until sugar dissolves. Set aside to cool slightly. Glaze rugelach with a pastry brush right out of the oven. They are best eaten hot, fresh out of the oven!

Tip

These cookies are best served right out of the oven, but you can also keep them in an airtight container for up to three days and reheat in a 250°F/120°C oven. If you don't have a stand mixer, you can make these by hand; they just take more time to knead.

Strawberry Rosewater Hamantaschen

Prep time: 1 hour 30 minutes • Inactive prep time: overnight • Cook time: 55 minutes • Makes: 20 cookies

There is an old joke about Jewish holidays that goes "They tried to kill us, we won, let's eat!" And Purim is no exception. It's customary to make triangular cookies called hamantaschen, filled with poppy seeds, jam, or prunes, to represent the fashionable three-cornered hat Haman was known to sport. This dough is a great base for your favorite fillings.

For jam

1 pound (455 g) fresh strawberries, washed, hulled, and quartered
1 cup (200 g) granulated sugar
1 tablespoon rosewater
1 teaspoon vanilla extract

For dough

1 stick or ½ cup (113 g) unsalted butter, softened
¾ cup (150 g) granulated sugar
½ teaspoon vanilla extract
2 tablespoons orange juice
1 whole egg plus 1 egg for egg wash
2 cups (284 g) all-purpose flour
1 teaspoon baking powder
¼ teaspoon kosher salt
1 tablespoon water

1. First, make the jam. Place strawberries in a medium stockpot and soften while stirring over medium-high heat, about 5 minutes. Then add sugar, rosewater, and vanilla and bring to a boil while stirring; lower to a simmer and simmer for 30 minutes or until thick, stirring occasionally. Skim off any impurities and mash strawberries. Remove from heat and cool; the jam will continue to thicken as it cools. At this point you can use the jam or it will keep in the refrigerator for up to 2 weeks.

2. Now it's cookie time! In a large bowl, beat butter and sugar together with a hand or stand mixer with whisk attachment until light and fluffy, about 2–3 minutes. You can do this by hand, too.

3. Then add vanilla and orange juice and beat until combined. Add 1 egg and beat until combined.

4. In a medium bowl, whisk together flour, baking powder, and salt. Add the flour mixture to the wet ingredients and mix by hand just until combined. Form dough into a ball, flatten slightly, wrap in plastic wrap, and refrigerate overnight. You can also freeze dough for up to 2 months.

5. On a lightly floured surface with a lightly floured with a rolling pin, roll out the dough about $1/8$-inch (3 mm) thick. If your dough cracks, let it warm up a bit more. Then, using a 3-inch (7.5 cm) round cookie cutter (or wine glass!), cut out cookies. Place 1 teaspoon jam (no more or it will leak) into the center of each circle, and fold over the 3 sides, pinching or overlapping, to form a triangle. Use the scraps to roll out more hamantaschen dough. Place hamantaschen on 2 parchment paper–lined baking sheets 1 inch (2.5 cm) apart.

6. Preheat oven to 350°F/180°F with 2 oven racks in the middle of the oven. Whisk egg for wash with water and lightly brush over hamantaschen. Freeze for 30 minutes. Then bake for 15–20 minutes or until golden brown on the bottom. Cool for 5 minutes on the baking sheet, and then finish cooling on a cooling rack. Store in an airtight container for up 5 days or freeze for up to 2 months.

Tip

If you are having trouble rolling the dough out, let the dough warm up slightly. Also, make sure to roll your dough thin, as thick dough may spread in the oven.

Chocolate Halva Hamantaschen

Prep time: 1 hour 30 minutes • Inactive prep time: overnight • Cook time: 15 minutes • Makes: 20 cookies

This version of hamantaschen indulges my love for chocolate, with a little Israeli twist. Right in the middle of working on this cookbook, I was invited to go on a trip to Israel. Anyone who has been to Jerusalem has probably been to the Mahane Yehuda Market, often referred to as "The Shuk," and probably remembers those huge hunks of halva—flaky, dense tahini and sugar candy that is weirdly addicting. The Shuk was very crowded that day—it was the Friday before a holiday—but I was able to get close enough to try a chocolate halva chunk. And so a new hamantaschen flavor was born.

For dough

1 stick or ½ cup (113 g) unsalted
　butter, softened
¾ cup (150 g) granulated sugar
½ teaspoon vanilla extract
2 tablespoons orange juice
1 whole egg plus 1 egg for egg wash
2 cups (284 g) all-purpose flour
¼ cup (22 g) unsweetened cocoa
　powder, plus more for rolling out
　dough
1 teaspoon baking powder
¼ teaspoon kosher salt
1 tablespoon water
Sesame seeds, for garnish

For filling

½ cup (120 ml) heavy cream
3 tablespoons unsalted butter
4 ounces (114 g) semisweet
　chocolate, chopped
¼ cup (60 g) tahini paste
1 teaspoon vanilla extract
1 tablespoon all-purpose flour
1 egg yolk

1. First, make the dough. In a large bowl or stand mixer, beat butter and sugar together until light and fluffy, about 2–3 minutes.

2. Add vanilla and orange juice and beat until combined. Then add egg and beat until combined.

3. In a medium bowl, whisk together flour, cocoa powder, baking powder, and salt. Add the flour mixture to the wet ingredients and mix by hand just until combined. Form dough into a ball, flatten slightly, wrap in plastic wrap, and refrigerate overnight. You can also freeze it for up to 2 months.

4. Make the filling. In a small saucepan, heat cream and butter over medium heat while stirring until butter is melted. Remove from heat, mix in chocolate, and stir to melt and incorporate. Add tahini, vanilla, flour, and egg yolk and combine. Let cool, and refrigerate to set at least 2–3 hours.

5. When ready to bake, on a lightly cocoa-powdered surface (you can use flour but it may color the dough) with a lightly cocoa-powdered (or floured) rolling pin, roll out the dough to about 1/8-inch (3 mm) thick. Using a 3-inch (7.5 cm) round cookie cutter (or wine glass), cut out circles. Place 1 teaspoon of filling into the center of each circle and fold over the three sides, overlapping, to form a triangle. Place hamantaschen 1 inch (2.5 cm) apart on 2 parchment paper–lined baking sheets.

6. Freeze for 30 minutes to prevent spreading. Preheat oven to 350°F/180°F with 2 oven racks in the middle of the oven. Whisk egg for wash with water and lightly brush over hamantaschen. Sprinkle with sesame seeds.

7. Then bake for 12–15 minutes or until golden brown on the bottom. Cool for 5 minutes on the baking sheet, and then finish cooling on a cooling rack.

Tip

If you are having trouble rolling the dough out, let the dough warm up slightly. Also, make sure to roll your dough thin, as thick dough may spread in the oven.

Black and Pink Cookies

Prep time: 45 minutes • Cook time: 15 minutes • Makes: 10–12 cookies

Look to the cookie! (*Seinfeld*, anyone?). Traditionally, this lemony-flavored drop cookie has more of a cakey texture, with half chocolate, half vanilla frosting. Everyone has their own way of eating one: Some eat the black side first, some the white side, while others go right down the middle. There really is no wrong way, though my vote goes to alternating one bite of each. These are moist with the perfect hint of lemon, and a naturally pink raspberry frosting takes things up a notch.

For cookies

½ cup or 1 stick (113 g) unsalted butter, softened

1 cup (100 g) granulated sugar

1 egg, at room temperature

½ cup (115 g) sour cream

1 vanilla bean, scraped (or 2 teaspoons vanilla extract)

1 teaspoon lemon zest (from 1 lemon)

1 tablespoon lemon juice (from 1 lemon)

2¼ cups (254 g) cake flour

⅛ teaspoon kosher salt

1 teaspoon baking powder

½ teaspoon baking soda

For frostings

1 cup (110 g) fresh raspberries

⅓ cup (80 ml) water

1 tablespoon corn syrup

4 cups (452 g) powdered sugar

4 ounces (114 g) unsweetened chocolate, chopped

1. Preheat oven to 375°F/190°C with the oven racks in the middle of the oven.

2. In a large bowl with a stand mixer with a paddle attachment, or using a hand mixer, beat butter and sugar on medium speed until light and fluffy, about 3 minutes, making sure to scrape down the sides of bowl.

3. Add egg, sour cream, vanilla, lemon zest, and juice and beat just until smooth.

4. In a separate medium bowl, combine cake flour, salt, baking powder, and baking soda. Stir flour mixture into wet ingredients with a large spoon, a little at a time until combined. Dough should be thick and sticky.

5. Line 2 baking sheets with parchment paper, and scoop large (2 heaping tablespoons) spoonfuls 1 inch (2.5 cm) apart onto the sheet. Swirl to flatten slightly into 3-inch (7.5 cm) circles as these will not spread too much. Try to make them as round as possible by molding with your fingers. You can also place the dough in a 3-inch (7.5 cm) round cookie cutter to shape perfectly, though you'll have to smooth the edges even so. These are big, but not as big as NYC-sized cookies!

6. Bake for 12 minutes until the edges start to brown, rotating after 6 minutes. Cool for 5 minutes on the baking sheet and then finish cooling on cooling racks (at least 30 minutes).

7. Now it's frosting time! In a small saucepan, place raspberries, water, and corn syrup and bring to a boil. Lower to a simmer and simmer for 10 minutes, stirring occasionally. Place powdered sugar in a large heatproof bowl and set aside.

8. Strain the raspberry mixture to remove the seeds (you should have about ⅓ cup (80 ml) after it's strained) and add the mixture to the powdered sugar. Frosting should be thick but spreadable. If your frosting is very runny, add more powdered sugar. If it's very thick, add a little hot water.

9. Melt chocolate over a double boiler or in the microwave (heat for 15 seconds at a time until melted, stirring each time), and then place in a separate medium bowl and let cool. Mix in a little less than half of the raspberry frosting mixture to make the chocolate frosting. Add a little warm water if the frosting is too thick and powdered sugar if it is too runny. It should be thick but spreadable.

10. Frost each half of the flat side (the bottom) of cookies with raspberry frosting and then follow with the chocolate. Let the cookies dry on wax paper. Let harden before serving.

Tip

These cookies are best served the same day you bake them, but they can be stored in an airtight container between layers of wax paper for up to three days. Be sure to use cake flour for that light texture.

Espresso-Cherry Mandel Bread

Prep time: 30 minutes • Inactive prep time: 2 hours • Cook time: 50 minutes • Makes: about 36 cookies

Baking can be scary y'all, but this mandel bread is easy, delicious, and almost foolproof. Mandel bread, aka mandel brot, comes from the Yiddish, meaning almond bread. It's like a Jewish biscotti, but softer and still delicious with tea or coffee. Whiskey is optional.

For mandel bread

2 eggs

1 cup (235 ml) vegetable
   (or grape seed) oil

½ cup (115 g) full-fat sour cream

2 teaspoons vanilla extract

1 tablespoon orange zest
   (from 1 orange)

3 cups (426 g) all-purpose flour

1 cup (200 g) granulated sugar

1 teaspoon baking powder

2 teaspoons ground cardamom

1 tablespoon instant espresso powder

¼ teaspoon kosher salt

1 cup (125 g) slivered almonds, rough
   chopped

1 cup (150 g) dried cherries
   (if very big, rough chop these as well)

For chocolate dip

12 ounces (340 g) semisweet chocolate

1. In a large bowl of a stand mixer with paddle attachment, or using a hand mixer, beat eggs, oil, sour cream, vanilla, and zest on medium speed until combined.

2. In a separate large bowl, mix together flour, sugar, baking powder, cardamom, instant espresso, and salt; add to the wet ingredients and combine just until mixed. Stir in slivered almonds and cherries. Cover the dough and refrigerate for at least 2 hours or up to 24 hours. Dough will seem oily, but it will dissipate when cooked.

3. Preheat oven to 350°F/180°C with the racks in the center of the oven. Prep 2 baking sheets with parchment paper. Divide dough into 4 equal pieces and with wet hands form into 2 logs, about 3 x 7 inches (7.5 x 23 cm) in size, on each. Bake for 30 minutes, or until golden brown, rotating the pans halfway through baking.

4. Remove mandel bread from oven, let cool 5–10 minutes or until cool enough to slice, and carefully cut into 1-inch (2.5 cm) slices. Lower oven to 250°F/120°C.

5. Put the slices back on the baking sheets and bake an additional 10 minutes per side, or until crispy. Cool on a cooling rack.

6. Melt chocolate in a double boiler or microwave (heat for 15 seconds at a time until melted, stirring each time). Dip the ends of the mandel bread in chocolate and dry on parchment paper. You can also refrigerate the dipped mandel bread to help the chocolate harden faster.

Tip

Store cookies in an airtight container layered between wax paper for up to five days or three months in the freezer.

Pumpkin-Pecan Cinnamon Roll Strudel

Prep time: 1 hour • Inactive prep time: 2 hours • Cook time: 40 minutes • Makes: about 24 cookies

This spicy, pumpkiny recipe just screams fall. And it's perfect for the holiday of Sukkot when we build fancy huts called sukkahs out of branches and other natural materials to remind us of the ones our ancestors built by their crops every harvest season. There is definitely more than one way to make a strudel. My Bubbe, always used this richer butter and sour cream dough that I just love.

For dough

2½ cups (355 g) all-purpose flour

¼ cup (50 g) granulated sugar

1 cup (230 g) sour cream

2 sticks or 1 cup (225 g) unsalted butter, softened

For filling

⅔ cup (75 g) unsalted butter, softened

½ cup (75 g) canned or fresh puréed pumpkin

½ cup (100 g) granulated sugar, plus more for sprinkling

½ cup (115 g) dark or light brown sugar

1 tablespoon ground cinnamon, plus more for sprinkling

1¼ cups (125 g) pecans, chopped

½ teaspoon kosher salt

For icing

4 ounces (113 g) cream cheese, at room temperature

1 cup (113 g) powdered sugar

½ stick or ¼ cup (57 g) unsalted butter, softened

½ teaspoon vanilla extract

1 tablespoon whole milk

1. In a large bowl of a stand mixer with paddle attachment, or using a hand mixer, combine flour, sugar, sour cream, and butter until just combined. You can also mix dough by hand if desired. Turn dough out onto clean surface and knead for 5 minutes, or use a dough hook in the stand mixer until you have a shaggy, soft, slightly sticky dough. If the dough is too sticky to manage, add just a little more flour to help it roll into a ball.

2. Wrap dough in plastic wrap and refrigerate at least 2 hours or up to 3 days.

3. When ready to bake, preheat the oven to 350°F/180°C with 2 racks in the center of the oven. To make filling, mix together butter, pumpkin, sugars, cinnamon, and salt with a hand mixer or spoon in a medium bowl.

4. Divide dough in 2 pieces. On a lightly floured surface with a lightly floured rolling pin, roll each one into a very thin ⅛-inch-thick (3 mm) rectangle (the thinner the better, but careful not to let it stick) about 10 x 15 inches (25 x 38 cm).

5. Spread a thin layer of filling on the dough, leaving a ½-inch (1 cm) border on the edges.

6. Sprinkle half of the pecans and roll the dough up tightly like a jellyroll, starting from the longer side so you end up with a 15-inch-long (38 cm) roll. Secure the ends so the filling doesn't leak out (use a little water if your dough isn't sticking to itself) and place the roll seam-side down.

7. Sprinkle generously with cinnamon and sugar. Repeat with other roll and place on 2 parchment paper–lined baking sheets.

8. Bake for 35–40 minutes, rotating plans halfway through or until golden brown. Cool on cooling rack, and slice into 1½-inch-thick (3.5 cm) pieces. The filling should be gooey, but if it seems raw, lay slices flat on baking sheet and bake 5 minutes longer.

9. To make icing, combine cream cheese, powdered sugar, butter, and vanilla in medium bowl and beat with a hand or stand mixer until smooth. Add milk as needed to make a thick but pourable glaze. Drizzle on strudel.

Tip

If the roll doesn't fit
on the sheet, slightly
bend it like a rainbow
to make it fit.

Chocolate Ombré Layer Cookies

Prep time: 2 hours • Inactive prep time: 8 hours 45 minutes • Cook time: 30 minutes • Makes about 40 cookies

Jewish and Italian immigrants to America often lived in close proximity, so it makes sense that some food overlapped. While these cookies are usually the colors of the Italian flag, I made mine blue, perhaps in a subconscious nod to the Israeli flag. These cookies take time, but are totally worth it. Now, who can I interest in a prune cannoli?

For cookies

1 (8-ounce) can almond paste
  (1 cup/228 g) (some are 7 ounces;
  that works too)
1 cup (200 g) granulated sugar, divided
2½ sticks or 1¼ cups (282 g) unsalted
  butter, softened
4 eggs, separated
1 teaspoon almond extract
1 tablespoon lemon juice (from ½–1
  lemon)
1 teaspoon lemon zest (from 1 lemon)
2 cups (282 g) all-purpose flour
½ teaspoon kosher salt
Food coloring (I use gel turquoise, but
  use what you like)
2 (12-ounce/355 ml) jars smooth
  apricot preserves (about 2
  tablespoons per layer)

For ganache

8 ounces (227 g) bittersweet
  chocolate, chopped
½ cup (120 ml) heavy cream

1. Preheat oven to 350°F/180°C and set 2 racks in middle. Grease three 12 x 8-inch (30 x 20 cm) baking pans and line bottoms with parchment paper, letting paper drape over the shorter pan sides. (If you only have 2 baking pans, it's fine; you'll just have to bake more times.)

2. In a large bowl of a stand mixer with the paddle attachment, or with a hand mixer, beat together almond paste and ¾ cup (150 g) sugar until well blended and you have a crumbly dough, about 2–3 minutes. Add butter and beat until pale and fluffy, about 2–3 additional minutes. Add egg yolks, one at a time, then add almond extract, lemon juice, and zest and beat until combined well, about 2 minutes. Reduce speed to low, then add flour and salt and mix until just combined.

3. In a separate large bowl of a stand mixer with a whisk attachment or a hand mixer beat whites at medium-high speed until they just hold soft peaks. Add remaining ¼ cup (50 g) sugar, a little at a time, beating at high speed until you have stiff, slightly shiny peaks.

4. Fold egg white mixture into almond mixture and divide batter into 5 bowls. Stir some food coloring into the first bowl, and then a little less into each subsequent bowl so it fades from darkest to lightest. Pour batter (1 color into each of the three remaining pans, you'll have 2 or 3 bowls of batter remaining) into prepared pans, and spread with a spatula to even out. Cover the other bowls of batter until ready to use to prevent a hard layer from forming. The batter in the pans will be very thin.

5. Bake the first 2 or 3 layers 6–8 minutes, until just set and the edges are turning brown. They will look slightly undercooked.

6. Let cake cool slightly in the pans and then, using paper overhang, transfer cake layers to cooling racks to cool, about 15 minutes, being sure not to overlap layers or they will stick. Clean cool pans, then butter and line pans and repeat with remaining batter.

7. While layers are cooking, heat the apricot preserves in a small saucepan over medium until runny. Strain to remove any chunks and let cool.

8. When all layers are cool, invert lightest colored layer onto a parchment or wax paper–lined large baking sheet. Discard paper and spread with a thin layer of preserves, about 1½–2 tablespoons. Invert the next lightest color on top of that layer, discarding paper. Spread with more preserves. Repeat with other layers, ending with cake (not jam).

9. Cover with plastic wrap and chill at least 8 hours or up to overnight.

10. Remove plastic wrap and bring layers to room temperature. Trim the edges of with a long serrated knife to even out.

11. To make the ganache, place chocolate in a medium heatproof bowl and set aside. Heat cream in a small saucepan just until it simmers, then pour over chocolate. Mix together until chocolate is melted and ganache is smooth.

12. Spread half of chocolate in a thin layer on top of the cake. You can also glaze the sides if you like too. Work quickly so chocolate does not set before you smooth it out. Refrigerate, uncovered, until chocolate is set, about 15 minutes. Then cover the cake with another sheet of wax paper, place another baking sheet on top, flip over, and remove paper. Spread with remaining chocolate. Freeze until firm, about 30 minutes.

13. Cut lengthwise into 4 strips (or more) and then cut across to make 1-inch (2.5 cm) cookies. Serve at room temperature.

Lemon Mohn Sandwich Cookies

Prep time: 40 minutes • Inactive prep time: 2 hours • Cook time: 15 minutes • 30 sandwich cookies

As I was developing recipes for this book, my Bubbe said I had to include her favorite Mohn cookies. Mohn is the Yiddish word for poppy seeds. They have a nutty flavor, and a buttery yet crunchy texture. While great on their own, they're even better in an adorable sandwich form.

For cookies

3 cups (426 g) all-purpose flour
²/₃ cup (45 g) poppy seeds
2 teaspoons baking powder
¼ teaspoon kosher salt
2 sticks or 1 cup (225 g) unsalted
   butter, softened
²/₃ cup (133 g) granulated sugar, plus
   more for sprinkling
1 egg, plus 1 egg for egg wash
1 tablespoon water
1 teaspoon vanilla extract
1 tablespoon lemon zest (from about
   4 lemons)
¼ cup (60 ml) lemon juice (from about
   4 lemons)

For filling

1 stick or ½ cup (113 g) unsalted
   butter, at room temperature
1 teaspoon lemon zest (from 1 lemon)
1 tablespoon lemon juice (from 1
   lemon)
3 cups (339 g) powdered sugar

1. In a large bowl, stir together flour, poppy seeds, baking powder, and salt. Set aside.

2. In a separate large bowl, using a hand or stand mixer with whisk attachment, beat butter and sugar on medium speed until light and fluffy, about 2–3 minutes. Add in egg, vanilla, lemon zest, and lemon juice and beat until combined.

3. Fold flour mixture into sugar mixture and mix with your hands until a dough forms. It may look like it won't come together, but it will!

4. Divide the dough in 2 pieces and form into logs, about 2 inches (5 cm) in diameter. Wrap in plastic wrap and refrigerate for 2 hours or up to overnight.

5. Meanwhile, make the filling. Mix together butter, lemon zest, and lemon juice in a small bowl. Add in powdered sugar and mix until you have a thick, spreadable frosting.

6. When ready to bake, preheat oven to 350°F/180°C. Line 2 baking sheets with parchment paper and set aside. Set the baking racks in the center of the oven.

7. Slice the logs into very thin, ⅛-inch-thick (3 mm) cookies, smoothing the edges if needed. Beat remaining egg and water in a small bowl; brush cookies with egg wash, and sprinkle with sugar (you can also use coarse sugar for more crunch).

8. Bake 10–15 minutes, until lightly golden brown. Cool on the cookie sheet for 5 minutes, then finish cooling on cooling racks.

9. Once completely cool, spread a heaping teaspoon of filling on a cookie and top with a second cookie. Store cookies in an airtight container for up to five days.

Tip
Call your local bagel shop and ask to buy poppy seeds from them. They may even give you some for free!

Cakes and Breads

Even though my birthday is in January, I became a Bat Mitzvah in May, since brunch tents and pastel blue suits (with coordinating nails) do not play well with Connecticut winters. So I had the privilege of having my Torah portion be the Ten Commandments. Definitely an important one, and even my thirteen-year-old self thought it was pretty cool. That was until it was time to practice the English version. You would think the Hebrew would be the trickier part, but not when I got to the commandment to "not covet thy neighbor's ass." Ass, as in donkey. As in what they have but you don't. I thought I was mature; I could get through saying "ass" in front of a few hundred people. No problem. That is until my ten-year-old brother chimed in: "No matter how shapely it is, or how many 'Buns of Steel' videos they did." Hey, this was the 90s. And, of course, on the big day I burst into a huge fit of giggles. Luckily, I think all was forgotten by the time we were dancing to the *Macarena* at the after party and diving into my rainbow sprinkle (very grown-up) bat mitzvah cake.

Tzimmes Cake

Prep time: 30 minutes • Inactive prep time: 30 minutes • Cook time: 45 minutes • Makes: 16 servings

Tzimmes, a medieval German stew of vegetables, fruit, and meat, wasn't always as sweet as we know it today. We can thank our American relatives for that change. I added traditional sweet potatoes, carrots, and (boozy) raisins to yield a super-moist, slightly spicy cake perfect for a sweet Rosh Hashanah. Tzimmes means "to make a fuss over" in Yiddish, but this cake is so easy, it's no fuss at all. Don't be intimidated by the ingredient list; you probably have most of these items in your pantry already.

For cake

Butter, oil, or cooling spray for greasing pan
½ cup (75 g) raisins
½ cup (120 ml) amaretto (whiskey also works nicely)
1½ cups (170 g) all-purpose flour, plus more for flouring the pan
1 teaspoon baking powder
½ teaspoon baking soda
1 tablespoon ground cinnamon
1 teaspoon ground allspice
1 teaspoon ground ginger
½ teaspoon kosher salt
½ cup (115 g) packed light or dark brown sugar
½ cup (100 g) granulated sugar
½ cup (115 g) sour cream
½ cup (120 ml) vegetable oil (grape seed or canola)
½ cup (120 ml) orange juice
1 teaspoon vanilla extract
2 eggs, at room temperature
½ cup (165 g) cooked sweet potato flesh, cooled (from 1 small sweet potato: cook in a 400°F/205°C oven for 1 hour or until tender, or zap in the microwave for 7–8 minutes)
1 cup (120 g) shredded carrots (about 2 medium carrots)
½ cup (50 g) pecans, chopped

For glaze

½ stick or ¼ cup (55 g) unsalted butter
1/3 cup (75 g) light brown sugar (dark brown will yield a slightly darker glaze)
1/3 cup (80 ml) heavy whipping cream
1 teaspoon vanilla extract
1 teaspoon ground cinnamon
1 cup (113 g) powdered sugar

1. Preheat oven to 350°F/180°C. Lightly grease a 12-cup (2.8 L) Bundt pan with butter and a dusting of flour (or use nonstick spray) and set aside.

2. Combine raisins with amaretto in a small bowl. Let marinate for 30 minutes, mixing periodically, then drain raisins and set aside. You can skip this step and just add dry raisins if you want a booze-free cake.

3. In a medium bowl, whisk together flour, baking powder, baking soda, cinnamon, allspice, ginger, and salt.

4. In a large bowl, with a stand mixer with whisk attachment, hand mixer, or hand whisk, mix together sugars, sour cream, oil, orange juice, and vanilla.

5. Add eggs to sugar mixture one at a time. Then mix in sweet potato (switch to a spoon if mixing by hand). Mix until uniform and mostly smooth. It's okay if the sweet potatoes are not completely incorporated; those little chunks will be moist and delicious. Gradually add flour mixture, stirring until just combined. Then stir in carrots, nuts, and amaretto-soaked raisins.

6. Pour batter into the Bundt pan and bake for about 45 minutes or until golden brown and a toothpick inserted in the center of the cake comes out clean. Let cool 10 minutes in the pan, and then transfer to a cooling rack to finish cooling.

7. To make the icing, combine butter, brown sugar, cream, vanilla, and cinnamon in a small saucepan over medium heat until butter is completely melted and sugar is dissolved, about 3–5 minutes, being careful not to let mixture burn. Remove from heat and cool completely. Then whisk in powdered sugar until smooth. Drizzle or pour over cooled cake.

Tip

This cake actually gets better and moister as it sits; it can be made up to three days before serving. Frost right before serving.

Blueberry-Lemon Cheesecake with Pretzel Crust

Prep time: 1 hour 20 minutes • Inactive prep time: 8+ hours • Cook time: 1 hour • Makes: 12 servings

Shavuot is the holiday that recognizes the Israelites receiving the Ten Commandments on Mount Sinai. We tend to eat dairy on this holiday: blintzes, kugel, and cheesecake. Jewish cheesecake once contained curd cheese, and was not the light, creamy dessert we know today. Then those smart kids in New York took the traditional recipe and swapped it out for cream cheese, making it tangy, creamy, and irresistible. When I first thought about the curd cheese, lemon curd popped into my mind. And blueberries, because they're a perfect match with lemon. Salty crunchy pretzels balance everything out perfectly.

For crust

2 cups crushed pretzels
   (measure after crushing)
¼ cup (75 g) light brown sugar
6 tablespoons unsalted butter, melted

For filling

4 (8-ounce 910 g) packages cream cheese, at room temperature and cut into chunks
1 cup (200 g) granulated sugar
Pinch kosher salt
½ cup (115 g) full-fat sour cream, at room temperature
4 eggs, at room temperature
2 teaspoons lemon juice (from 1 lemon)
1 teaspoon lemon zest (from 1 lemon)
1 teaspoon vanilla extract
1 pint (2 cups/290 g) blueberries, washed and dried well

1. Preheat oven to 350°F/180°C, and place a rack in the lower third of the oven.

2. First, start by preparing the spring form pan. Wrap the outside of the pan in a large piece of heavy-duty foil and fold over the sides by ½ inch (1 cm), making sure to secure. Repeat with another piece of foil and a third if you are crazy like me. The foil will protect your crust from the water bath, which helps the cheesecake bake gently and evenly.

3. To make the crust, pulse the pretzels in a food processor until fine. If you don't have a food processor, place them in a plastic bag and crush with a rolling pin until pulverized. Then in a medium bowl, combine pulverized pretzels with sugar and incorporate the butter evenly with a spoon or your hands.

4. Press the crust into the bottom of the pan, making sure there are not any holes. Bake for 10 minutes, let cool completely, and lower oven temperature to 325°F/170°C.

5. To make the filling, cream the cream cheese in an electric stand mixer with a paddle attachment, or use a hand mixer on medium-high speed for 3 minutes, or until very creamy. Make sure to use a spatula to scrape down the sides periodically so everything is evenly blended.

6. To the same bowl, add sugar and salt and beat another 3 minutes, scraping as needed to get everything incorporated. Add sour cream and combine.

7. Then add eggs, one at a time, and beat to combine after each addition. Scrape again with the spatula as needed. You want everything incorporated and whipped to perfection! Lastly, beat in lemon juice, zest, and vanilla. Gently stir in blueberries.

8. Put the spring form pan in a roasting pan with high sides, and pour the batter on top of the crust, shaking the pan a little to even out the batter. Boil water and fill the roasting pan halfway up the sides of the spring form. Place on the lower rack of the oven. (You can also pour the water in the pan after placing it in the oven, but be careful either way! Please don't burn yourself, says Bubbe.) Bake for 60 minutes, or until cheesecake is firm but still a little jiggly. Crack the oven door slightly (secure with a large spoon if it doesn't stay open on its own) and

For lemon curd

2 teaspoons lemon zest (from 1 lemon)

⅓ cup (80 ml) fresh lemon juice (from 2 lemons)

½ cup (100 g) granulated sugar

3 egg yolks

½ stick or ¼ cup (55 g) unsalted butter, cut into small pieces

For garnish

½ cup (73 g) blueberries, or more if needed

Zest of 1 lemon

Powdered sugar

Edible flowers (optional)

Tip

Make a day or two before you plan to serve to give the cheesecake time to cool and set. Chilled cheesecake is much easier to cut evenly. Slice it with a large knife that you run under hot water and wipe clean between slices.

turn off the oven. Let the cheesecake cool this way for an hour. This will help the cake cool evenly and prevent cracks. If you get a few cracks, don't worry; we are covering this baby with lemon curd! Cover the cooled cheesecake with foil and refrigerate overnight.

9. Make the lemon curd. In a small saucepan over medium heat, whisk together lemon zest, juice, and sugar until sugar dissolves. Get a small saucepan of simmering water ready for a double boiler.

10. Whisk egg yolks in a heatproof bowl and temper in the lemon mixture by adding 1 spoonful at a time (so as to not cook eggs) until combined. Strain the mixture through a fine-mesh strainer and return it to the heatproof bowl.

11. Place the bowl over the saucepan of simmering water over medium heat, making sure the water does not touch the bowl. Cook, while stirring, until the curd is thick enough to coat the back of a spoon. Make sure it never reaches a boil. Remove from heat and stir in butter until fully incorporated. Let cool and refrigerate.

12. When the curd is cool, pour it evenly over the cooled cheesecake, cover in plastic wrap, and refrigerate 1 hour until set or overnight. A well-chilled cheesecake is easier to cut evenly.

13. When ready to serve, carefully run a knife around the inside edge of the pan and remove the spring form side. Garnish with blueberries, lemon zest, powdered sugar, and edible flowers, if desired.

Apricot and Fig-Stuffed Challah

Prep time: 1 hour 45 minutes • Inactive prep time: 5 hours • Cook time: 50 minutes Makes: 2 challot (that's the plural of challah!)

You are probably familiar with challah, the eggy braided bread that is served on Shabbat and holidays, and that makes a killer French toast. The secret to really awesome challah? Time. And yeast. And eggs. And bread flour. Okay, there are a few secrets. You can use this basic recipe for all your challah needs, stuffed or unstuffed. Want it less sweet for savory fillings? Leave out the honey and start with six cups of flour instead of seven.

For challah

2 tablespoons active dry yeast

1½ cups (355 ml) warm water (about 110°F/43°C)

½ cup (100 g) plus 2 teaspoons granulated sugar

2 whole eggs and 6 egg yolks, whisked, plus 1 extra yolk for glazing (save the whites for the Chocolate-Mint Meringue Cake or a hearty omelet!)

½ cup (120 ml) vegetable oil, plus more for greasing bowl

½ cup (120 ml) honey (trick: measure honey after oil and it will slide right out of the measuring cup)

1 tablespoon vanilla extract

2 teaspoons kosher salt

7–8 cups (995–1,135 g) bread flour

Raw sugar for garnish

For filling

1½ cups (224 g) dried mission figs

1½ cups (195 g) dried apricots

¾ cup (175 ml) orange juice

¾ cup (175 ml) honey

1 teaspoon ground cinnamon

¼ teaspoon ground nutmeg

¼ teaspoon ground allspice

1½ teaspoons vanilla extract

½ teaspoon kosher salt

1. First, make your challah dough. Prepare the yeast in a large mixing bowl for a stand mixer by whisking it with warm water and 2 teaspoons sugar (that helps activate the yeast). Let stand until it foams and puffs up, about 10 minutes. If it doesn't get foamy, your yeast is either bad or the water was too warm or cool. Try again!

2. Using the whisk attachment for the stand mixer, mix the remaining sugar, eggs, oil, honey, and vanilla into the yeast mixture. (You can use a whisk if you're doing this by hand.) Then add salt and combine. Gradually add 7 cups (995 g) flour, either using a hook attachment with the stand mixer on medium speed or a spoon and your hands until the dough begins to pull away from the sides. Dough should still be sticky. Knead for about 5–10 minutes, and then finish kneading by hand on a clean surface until dough is smooth and elastic. Form into a ball. If dough is too sticky to handle, add a bit more flour, but it should be soft, smooth, and slightly tacky—not dry.

3. Place the dough in a bowl greased with oil and cover. Let dough rise in a warm place until it has at least doubled in size, about 2–3 hours. I put mine on top of an oven heated to the lowest temperature.

4. Meanwhile, make the apricot and fig filling. In a small saucepan, combine figs, apricots, orange juice, honey, spices, vanilla, and salt. Bring to a simmer over medium heat and cook, stirring occasionally, until the figs and apricots are soft and the liquid thickens, about 15 minutes. Remove from heat, let cool slightly, and process in a food processor until you have a paste. Set aside.

5. Now, time to braid! Place the dough on a lightly floured surface and punch down. Divide the dough in half, and keep one half covered. Divide each half into 3 equal pieces, and roll them out into 14 x 4-inch (36 x 10 cm) rectangles, about 1/8-inch (3 mm) thick. Alternatively, make 12 x 6-inch (30 x 15 cm) rectangles if you want more swirls rather than chunks of filling. If your dough keeps bouncing back, let it rest a bit. Spread ¼ cup of filling on each strand and roll each one up tightly from the long end, not letting in any air, securing with the other end to make sure no filling leaks out. Repeat with other strands.

6. Secure the three strands together at one end and braid until you reach the other end, then tuck the ends underneath the challah to secure. Repeat with other half of the dough.

7. Carefully place the loaves on 2 parchment paper–lined baking sheets, cover lightly with plastic wrap, and let rise for 1½ hours or until more than doubled in size. Challah should seem light.

8. Meanwhile, preheat oven to 350°F/180°C. Whisk last egg yolk and generously brush 2 coats over challah. Sprinkle with raw sugar. Bake for 30–35 minutes, or until golden brown and with an internal temperature of 190°F/88°C, rotating pans halfway through. If the challah start to brown too fast, cover with foil until done.

Tip

Definitely use the bread flour; it activates more gluten for that stringy pull-apart goodness we want in our challah. If you don't have a stand mixer, you can mix by hand as well. Challah is best served the day it's made, but leftover is awesome as croutons and French toast.

Coffee Coffee-Cake Muffins

Prep time: 30 minutes • Cook time: 25 minutes • Makes: 12 muffins

The original recipe for Jewish coffee cake actually did have coffee in it. So I added it back, in the form of espresso powder in the streusel. With tons of rich sour cream, these muffins make a great Yom Kippur break fast addition or Shavuot snack.

For muffins

²/₃ cup (150 g) full-fat sour cream
1 egg, at room temperature
½ teaspoon vanilla
1½ cups (213 g) all-purpose flour
¾ cup (150 g) granulated sugar
1½ tablespoons baking powder
½ teaspoon kosher salt
1 stick or ½ cup (113 g) unsalted
    butter, melted and cooled

For streusel

¾ cup (107 g) all-purpose flour
¼ cup (50 g) granulated sugar
½ cup (50 g) light brown sugar
1 tablespoon ground cinnamon
1½ tablespoons instant espresso
    powder
½ stick ¼ cup or (55 g) unsalted
    butter, melted and cooled

1. Preheat oven to 350°F/180°C. Line a 12-cup muffin tin with liners and set aside.

2. In a large bowl of a stand mixer with whisk attachment or with a hand mixer, beat sour cream, egg, and vanilla just until combined. In a separate medium bowl, combine flour, sugar, baking powder, and salt.

3. Add dry ingredients to egg mixture and beat just until combined. Then beat in butter just until combined.

4. Spoon batter evenly among the liners; they should each be two-thirds full.

5. To make streusel, combine flour, sugars, cinnamon, and espresso in a medium bowl. Then add butter and mix together with a spoon or your hands until crumbly.

6. Top each muffin evenly and generously with streusel, reserving some for touch-ups.

7. Bake muffins for 25 minutes. Halfway through baking, add more streusel if you want your muffins completely covered (the batter will rise as it bakes, leaving some empty spots.)

8. Cool muffins in the pan for 10 minutes, then remove and finish cooling on cooling rack.

Tip

You can make these by hand if you don't have an electric mixer. Keep leftover muffins in an airtight container for up to five days.

Cranberry-Walnut Challah Bread Pudding with White Chocolate–Thyme Sauce

Prep time: 30 minutes • Cook time: 50 minutes • Makes: 10–12 servings

Challah is one of my go-to comfort foods, so this rich challah bread pudding with an earthy white chocolate–thyme sauce is like comfort food on crack. As one recipe tester said: "Your bread pudding has changed my life. It's bright and flavorful and I want it all the time forever. I will make it as often as I can rationalize it." The secret ingredient is love, of course. And butter and cream, but mostly love.

For bread pudding

- 1 cup (150 g) walnuts
- 6 eggs, at room temperature
- 2 cups (475 ml) whole milk, at room temperature
- 2 cups (475 ml) heavy whipping cream, at room temperature
- 1½ cups (340 g) dark or light brown sugar
- ½ cup or 1 stick (112 g) unsalted butter, melted and cooled, plus more for greasing pan
- 1½ teaspoons vanilla extract
- 1 tablespoon orange zest
- 1 teaspoon ground cinnamon
- ½ teaspoon kosher salt
- 10 cups stale challah (at least a day old), diced into ½- to 1-inch (1–2.5 cm) chunks
- ½ cup (75 g) dried cranberries

For sauce

- 8 ounces (225 g) white chocolate, broken into chunks
- ¾ cup (175 ml) heavy whipping cream
- 5 large springs fresh thyme

1. Preheat oven to 350°F/180°C. Grease a 9 x 13-inch (23 x 33 cm) ceramic or glass baking pan and set aside. Place walnuts on a foil-lined cookie sheet and toast for 5 minutes or until browned and fragrant. Cool and rough-chop walnuts, setting aside half for garnish.

2. In a large bowl, whisk eggs together with a hand mixer, stand mixer with whisk attachment, or by hand. Then add milk and cream and blend. Add brown sugar, butter, vanilla, orange zest, cinnamon, and salt and blend until combined.

3. Add challah pieces, dried cranberries, and ½ cup walnuts to the liquid mixture and stir to combine. Let sit for 5 minutes or so to soak up the liquid.

4. Pour mixture into the greased baking pan and bake for 45 minutes or until brown and springy. Let rest for 15 minutes.

5. While challah bread pudding is baking, make white chocolate–thyme sauce. Put white chocolate pieces in a medium heat-resistant bowl. In a small saucepan, bring cream and thyme to a boil, lower to a simmer, and simmer for 5 minutes while stirring. Strain over chocolate and mix until all the chocolate is melted. Serve warm or at room temperature with warm or room-temperature bread pudding and more toasted walnuts.

Tip

If you don't have day-old challah, cut challah into cubes and toast in a 275°F/140°C oven for 10 minutes. Reheat one- to two-day-old bread pudding, covered, in a 250°F/120°C oven for 15 minutes, or until warm.

Peanut Butter and Dark Chocolate Babka

Prep time: 1 hour 15 minutes • Inactive prep time: 24 hours • Cook time: 30 minutes • Makes: 2 babkas

As my TV spirit character Elaine Benes says, "You can't beat a babka." This rich, yeasted bread is filled, in this case, with pretty much the best flavor combination of all time. No, I'm not talking about your morning coffee and whiskey. It's chocolate and peanut butter, with a touch of sea salt for good measure. The name babka comes from the Yiddish for grandmother, Bubbe. And given that I owe my love affair with Jewish food to my Bubbe, this cake is extra special to me.

For dough

2¼ teaspoons (1 packet) active dry yeast

½ cup (120 ml) warm whole milk (110°F/43°C), plus 1–2 more tablespoons, if needed

½ cup (100 g) granulated sugar, plus 2 teaspoons

4¼ cups (568 g) all-purpose flour, plus extra for dusting

½ tablespoon grated orange zest (from about ½ orange)

3 eggs, at room temperature

½ teaspoon kosher salt

1 stick or ½ cup (113 g) unsalted butter, cut into chunks and softened

Oil for greasing bowl (grape seed, sunflower, or vegetable oil)

For filling

1½ sticks or ¾ cup (169 g) unsalted butter

1½ cups (182 g) dark chocolate chips

1 cup (113 g) powdered sugar

¼ cup (22 grams) unsweetened cocoa powder

¼ teaspoon salt

1 cup (260 g) peanut butter (crunchy or smooth; I used smooth. Choose one that's easy to spread)

1. To make babka, combine yeast, milk, and 2 teaspoons sugar in a large bowl of a stand mixer and stir to dissolve. Wait 10 minutes; the mixture should get foamy and puff up. If it doesn't, the milk was probably too hot, too cold, or the yeast is dead. Try again!

2. Then add the flour, remaining sugar, and orange zest and stir to combine. Add eggs, one at a time, and mix with the dough hook attachment until dough comes together; this may take a couple of minutes.

3. With the mixer on low, add salt, then butter, a little at a time, mixing until incorporated. Then, mix dough on medium speed for about 8–10 minutes until completely smooth, shiny, and slightly sticky. Make sure to scrape down the sides as you mix so everything gets incorporated. Add more milk if it's dry.

4. Coat a large bowl with oil (you can just clean out your mixer bowl and use that) and place dough inside, cover with plastic, and refrigerate for 12–24 hours, or until almost doubled in size.

5. When the dough is ready, make the chocolate filling. Melt butter and chocolate together in a medium saucepan over low heat while stirring until smooth. Stir in powdered sugar, cocoa powder, and salt and let cool; mixture should form a spreadable paste.

6. Divide the dough in 2 equal pieces and roll out one piece into a very thin 16 x 12-inch (41 x 30 cm) rectangle. You may have to let the dough come to room temperature a bit if it is hard to roll.

7. Spread half of the chocolate filling over the dough, leaving a ½-inch (1 cm) border. Then top with half the peanut butter. Brush the farthest 12-inch (30 cm) end with water to help dough stick to itself. Then roll the dough up into a tight log using the shorter side so you have a 12-inch (30 cm) log. Place roll on a lightly floured baking sheet and refrigerate. Repeat with other dough and refrigerate both for 30 minutes.

8. Grease two 9 x 5-inch (23 x 13 cm) loaf pans with oil and line the bottoms with parchment paper. (To get a piece that fits perfectly, trace the bottom of the pan on the parchment paper and then cut out.)

For syrup

²/₃ cup (160 ml) water
²/₃ cup (133 g) granulated sugar
1 teaspoon flaked sea salt

Tip

Keep babkas wrapped tightly at room temperature for up to three days. Or freeze them for up to two months. You have leftovers? First of all, mazel tov for not polishing off the whole thing in one sitting. I like to mix babka chunks into vanilla ice cream.

9. Cut each log in half lengthwise and lay them next to each other. Pinch the top ends together and twist, keeping the cut sides up so you can see all the chocolate–peanut butter goodness. Place babka in the prepared loaf pan. Repeat with other loaf. Cover both with damp paper towels and let rise in a warm place another 1–2 hours. Alternatively, let rise in a refrigerator for 12 hours or overnight and bring to room temperature for 2–3 hours before baking.

10. Preheat oven to 375°F/190°C with a rack placed in the middle. Make the syrup by bringing water and sugar to a simmer until sugar dissolves. Remove from heat, and let it cool a bit.

11. Place a baking sheet on a rack below where cakes will bake to catch any drips. Bake loaves for 25–30 minutes, or until a thermometer reads 190°F/88°C. Halfway through baking, brush syrup all over babkas and return to the oven. Once babkas are done, immediately brush them with remaining syrup. Sprinkle with sea salt. Let cool in pan for 15 minutes, then remove and finish cooling on a cooling rack.

Apple Chai Cake with Maple Cream Cheese Drizzle

Prep time: 30 minutes • Cook time: 1 hour 15 minutes • Makes: 12 servings

It's hard to improve upon perfection. And my Bubbe's Jewish apple cake is pretty darn perfect. (Don't tell her I said this; her head is big enough as it is.) But I still gave it my personal spicy twist with chai-inspired ingredients and a maple–cream cheese drizzle. Because in the epic battle of cake vs. frosting, I'm team frosting every time. Apple cake is traditional for the Jewish New Year of Rosh Hashanah. We eat apples and honey to ensure a sweet coming year. I hope my year is sweet and spicy. Just like me.

For cake

Butter, oil, or cooking spray for greasing pan
3 cups (426 g) all-purpose flour, plus more for flouring the pan
1 tablespoon baking powder
1 teaspoon kosher salt
1 cup (235 ml) neutral-flavored oil (such as canola, vegetable, or grape seed)
4 eggs, at room temperature
¼ cup (60 ml) orange juice
1 tablespoon vanilla extract
2 cups (400 g) sugar, plus extra 5 tablespoons for apples
4–5 Granny Smith apples (3½ cups/440 g), sliced
1 tablespoon ground cardamom
1 teaspoon ground cinnamon
1 teaspoon ground ginger
1 teaspoon ground cloves

For drizzle

4 ounces (113 g) cream cheese, softened
2 tablespoons unsalted butter, softened
1 cup (113 g) powdered sugar
3 tablespoons maple syrup
Pinch kosher salt
1 tablespoon (plus 1–2 teaspoons, if needed) milk (or water or almond milk if keeping parve), at room temperature
¼ cup (25 g) walnuts, chopped

1. Preheat oven to 350ºF/ 180ºC. Grease a 12-cup (2.8 L) Bundt pan with butter and a dusting of flour (or use nonstick spray) and set aside.

2. In a large bowl, whisk together flour, baking powder, and salt. Set aside.

3. In a separate large bowl of a stand mixer with a whisk attachment, or in a large bowl with a hand mixer or spoon, mix together oil, eggs, orange juice, and vanilla. Then mix in sugar until combined. Add dry ingredients to wet ingredients, switching to the beater attachment (or continue to mix by hand). Mix until combined, being careful not to over mix. Batter should be thick but pourable.

4. Peel and core apples and cut into thin, ⅛-inch (3 mm) wedges.

5. Combine apples in a large bowl with remaining 5 tablespoons sugar, cardamom, cinnamon, ginger, and cloves.

6. Spoon a third of the batter in pan. Add half of the apple mixture in an even layer, add another third of the batter. Follow with other half apple mixture and last of the batter.

7. Bake for 1 hour 10 minutes or until toothpick comes out clean. Let cool in the pan for 15 minutes, then remove and finish cooling on a cooling rack.

8. To make drizzle, beat cream cheese and butter with a hand mixer until light and fluffy. Then beat in powdered sugar, butter, maple syrup, salt, and enough milk to get a thick but runny glaze. Keep beating until smooth. Drizzle all over your cooled cake and top with chopped walnuts.

Tip

This cake just gets better after a day or two! So feel free to make it ahead of time and frost just before serving.

Drunken Honey-Pomegranate Cake

Prep time: 30 minutes • Cook time: 1 hour • Makes: 12 servings

Sort of like the Jewish fruitcake, dry, sweet honey cake is usually not welcome at Rosh Hashanah, but it's always there. This version, however, is super-moist with coffee, pomegranate juice, and whiskey.

For cake

Butter, oil, or cooking spray for greasing pan

3 cups (426 g) all-purpose flour, plus more for flouring the pan

1 cup (200 g) granulated sugar

½ cup (115 g) light or dark brown sugar

2 teaspoons baking powder

1 teaspoon baking soda

½ teaspoon kosher salt

1 teaspoon ground ginger

1 tablespoon ground cardamom

1 teaspoon ground cinnamon

½ teaspoon ground nutmeg

1 cup (235 ml) canola oil (or vegetable or grape seed oil)

1 cup (235 ml) honey (trick: measure oil before honey and it will slide right out of the measuring cup)

3 eggs

1½ teaspoons vanilla extract

½ cup (120 ml) strong brewed coffee, at room temperature (can be decaf)

½ cup (120 ml) pomegranate juice

¼ cup (60 ml) whiskey (or more pomegranate juice; I've also used amaretto)

Zest from 1 lemon

For glaze

1 cup (113 g) powdered sugar

½ –1 tablespoon pomegranate juice

Pomegranate arils (seeds) for garnish

1. Preheat oven to 350°F/180°F. Grease 12-cup (2.8 L) Bundt pan and flour lightly.

2. In a large bowl, whisk together flour, sugars, baking powder, baking soda, salt, ginger, cardamom, cinnamon, and nutmeg until combined. Set aside.

3. In a separate large mixing bowl add oil, honey, eggs, vanilla, coffee, pomegranate juice, whiskey, and lemon zest and beat with a hand or stand mixer with a whisk attachment until incorporated. Add dry mixture to wet mixture and beat just until combined. You do not want to over-mix and make the cake tough. The batter should be thick but runny enough to stick to the whisk attachment.

4. Pour the batter into the prepared pan (it should fill two-thirds of the pan) and bake 50–60 minutes until cake is golden brown and a toothpick inserted into the cake comes out mostly clean.

5. Cool for 15 minutes in the pan and then turn the cake out onto a cooling rack to finish cooling.

6. To make glaze, whisk together powdered sugar and enough pomegranate juice to make a glaze thick enough to cover the back of a spoon. Drizzle over cake. Garnish with pomegranate arils and serve.

Tip

This cake just gets better after a day or two! Feel free to make it ahead of time and frost just before serving.

Snickerdoodle Bagels aka Unicorn Bagels

Prep time: 1 hour 30 minutes • Inactive Prep time: 2 hours • Cook time: 15 minutes • Makes: 8 large bagels

Is this recipe so wrong, or so wrong it's right? I'll let you be the judge. Growing up, Sundays were all about the bagels. I'd eat a poppy seed bagel with a schmear, usually sneaking a second half. What makes a bagel a bagel? The secret is in the boiling, which gives the bagel that irresistible crunchy outside and soft inside. These bagels have a crunchy cinnamon-sugar topping. It's not at all traditional, nor is it trying to be. The bagels are then filled with cookie dough–inspired cream cheese that's basically frosting in disguise.

For bagels

2 cups (475 ml) warm water (110°F/43°C), divided

2¼ teaspoons (1 packet) active dry yeast

4 tablespoons granulated sugar, divided, plus 1 cup (200 g) for sprinkling on bagels

5 cups (710 g) bread flour, plus more if needed

1 tablespoon cream of tartar

2 teaspoons kosher salt

1 tablespoon vegetable, canola, or grape seed oil, plus more for greasing the bowl

1 teaspoon vanilla extract

2 tablespoons ground cinnamon, plus 1 tablespoon for sprinkling on bagels

For boiling

4 quarts (3.8 l) water

1 cup (225 g) dark brown sugar

1. First, make the dough. Combine 1 cup (235 ml) warm water with yeast and 1 tablespoon sugar in the bowl of your stand mixer and let sit for 10 minutes until it bubbles up, foams, and doubles in size. If it doesn't, the water was too hot, too cold, or the yeast was old. Try again!

2. Then add 4 cups (568 g) flour, cream of tartar, salt, oil, vanilla, 2 tablespoons cinnamon, remaining 1 cup water, and 3 tablespoons sugar to the mix. Mix on low with a dough hook for 10–15 minutes until you have a smooth, firm dough. If dough is sticky, add a little flour; if it's a little dry, add a little more water. You may need more or less than 5 cups of flour.

3. Place the dough in a large bowl greased with oil, cover, and let rise in a warm place for 60–90 minutes, until doubled in size. I turn my oven on warm (200°F/93°C) and place the dough on top.

4. When dough is close to ready, bring a large stockpot filled with 4 quarts water and brown sugar (this adds flavor) to a boil. Then lower heat so it's barely simmering.

5. Preheat oven to 425°F/220°C.

6. Combine remaining 1 cup (200 g) granulated sugar with 1 tablespoon ground cinnamon for topping. (You can use more cinnamon if you want.) Line 2 baking sheets with parchment paper and set aside.

7. When dough is ready, punch it down and knead slightly for 1-2 minutes. Divide dough into 8 equal portions and roll into balls. Keep dough you aren't using covered with plastic wrap so it doesn't dry out. Make a hole in the center of each ball using your thumb and stretch to make the bagel hole. Place the bagels 2 inches (5 cm) apart on prepared baking sheets. Cover with plastic wrap and let rise for 15–20 minutes, or until they pass the float test. (What's the float test? Glad you asked! Fill a bagel-sized bowl with room-temperature water. Place a bagel in the bowl, and, if it floats, your bagels are ready to boil and bake. If the bagel does not float, check again every 5 minutes until it does.)

continued

For cream cheese

2 tablespoons unsalted butter

½ cup (115) light brown sugar

⅛ teaspoon kosher salt

8 ounces (227 g) cream cheese, softened

¼ cup (28 g) powdered sugar

1 teaspoon vanilla extract

½ cup (87g) semisweet mini chocolate chips

½ cup (13g) sprinkles (use long sprinkles, not round nonpareil as those can bleed)

8. Now it's time to boil and bake! Boiling your bagels gives them that crunchy outside and soft inside. Prepare a cooling rack. Boil bagels 3–4 at a time for 1 minute on each side and let dry on cooling rack. They should expand with boiling. Sprinkle tops immediately with cinnamon-sugar mixture, but resist the urge to cover both sides of the bagel, as this leads to a burnt caramel mess. Then place the bagels on baking sheets and bake for 13–15 minutes until golden, rotating halfway through baking.

9. While bagels are baking, make cream cheese. As mentioned earlier, this is frosting in disguise, but we are calling it cream cheese because it's for breakfast. In a small saucepan, melt butter, brown sugar, and salt over medium-low heat, stirring until the brown sugar dissolves. Remove from the heat and let cool. In a medium bowl, beat cream cheese, powdered sugar, and vanilla until light and fluffy, about 2–3 minutes. Then beat in butter mixture. Stir in chocolate chips and sprinkles. Cream cheese can be refrigerated for up to 5 days if you don't finish it with a spoon first.

Tip

These bagels are best the day they are made, but are still pretty tasty a day or two later. (Especially toasted. Don't tell the bagel police.) A note on the ingredients: Use bread flour if you can. It has more gluten and gives a better rise and a firmer chew. Cream of tartar adds the tanginess that makes a snickerdoodle cookie a snickerdoodle! If you don't have a stand mixer, you can make these by hand. It's tough but it will work!

Flourless (Pesach) Desserts

My Bubbe and mom plan the holiday menus literally months in advance. They make their shopping lists for Passover Seder in January. But I never kvetch, because the meal is always flawless. Everyone gathers in the kitchen slinging back Manischewitz, simmering matzah ball soup, and poking at the brisket. Is it done? Do you think it's done? Chewy brisket or dense matzah balls are not going to fly with my family. Of course everyone has a different opinion, but, in the end, it's always perfection. And just when you are too full to eat another bite, out come the desserts. Coconut macaroons, rich flourless chocolate cake, and those weird jelly things that no one claims to have brought and yet are always there. Next year, make room on the dessert table for a few more additions.

Flourless Chocolate-Orange Cupcakes with Beet Frosting

Prep time: 45 minutes • Cook time: 1 hour • Makes: 16 cupcakes

I hesitate to even call these cupcakes, because they are really more like individually portioned fudgy brownie pieces of heaven. I knew I wanted some sort of cupcake in this book since that is, in part, how my cooking journey got started. The swirled matzah bark adds a nice crunch to the rich cake and sweet, naturally pink frosting. Speaking of which, don't be scared of the beets: They mostly add color and not too much flavor.

For frosting

1 medium beet cleaned and trimmed
1 tablespoon lemon juice
2 sticks or 1 cup (225 g) unsalted butter, softened
8 ounces (227 g) cream cheese, softened
4 cups (450 g) powdered sugar
2 teaspoons vanilla extract

For matzah bark

3 pieces (84 g) matzah
1½ cups (182 g) semisweet chocolate chips
½ cup (85 g) white chocolate chips
Edible glitter (optional)

For cupcakes

1 stick or ½ cup (112 g) unsalted butter, softened
8 ounces (227 g) bittersweet chocolate
1 cup (200 g) granulated sugar
3 eggs
½ cup (43 g) unsweetened cocoa powder
1 teaspoon vanilla extract
¼ teaspoon kosher salt
1 tablespoon orange zest (from 1 orange)

1. First, cook the beet. Place beet in a medium saucepan and cover with water and lemon juice. Bring to a boil, lower to a simmer, and simmer for 30 minutes or until tender. Cool, peel, and shred beet with a grater; remove as much moisture as you can with paper towels. You should have about ½ cup (115g). Set aside.

2. Then, make matzah bark. Preheat oven to 350°F/180°C. Place matzah on a foil-lined cookie sheet with sides (jelly roll pan) or 9 x 12-inch (23 x 30 cm) cake pan and sprinkle semisweet chocolate chips evenly over matzah. You can break matzah into pieces if the whole pieces don't fit on your sheet.

3. Bake for 3–4 minutes to melt chocolate. Meanwhile, melt white chocolate in a small glass bowl in the microwave, 30 seconds at a time until melted, stirring after each interval.

4. Remove matzah from the oven, spread chocolate carefully with a knife to cover matzah, drizzle with white chocolate, and sprinkle with edible glitter, if using. If you'd like, you can also add other toppings at this point like coconut or slivered almonds.

5. Cool (in the refrigerator to speed things up, if desired) and then break matzah into pieces. Set aside. You'll have more than enough to use on the cupcakes. It makes a great snack!

6. Lower oven temperature to 300°F/150°C. Line a 12-cup cupcake pan and 4 cups of another pan with liners and set aside.

7. To make cupcakes, in a large saucepan over low heat, melt butter and chocolate, stirring occasionally.

8. In a separate bowl, beat sugar and eggs together for 2–3 minutes until very pale yellow. Remove chocolate from heat and stir in cocoa powder, vanilla, and salt. Add chocolate mixture to sugar mixture and mix to combine. Stir in orange zest.

9. Pour batter evenly into cupcake liners (1½ heaping tablespoons each) and bake for 25 minutes, just until set. Let cool in the pan for 10 minutes, then turn out and finish cooling on a wire rack. The cupcakes will sink a little as they cool.

10. To finish frosting, beat butter and cream cheese with a hand or stand mixer with whisk attachment in a large bowl until light and creamy. Then add powdered sugar and beat until combined. Add shredded beets and vanilla and beat until combined. This frosting makes a lot, so you can really pile it on.

11. Spread or pipe frosting (using a large-hole piping piece so the beet pieces can fit through) onto cooled cupcakes and top with a piece of matzah bark. Store leftovers in an airtight container in refrigerator for up to five days.

Tip
For the beet frosting, you can either purchase pre-cooked beets (I don't recommend canned) or cook your beet prior to making cupcakes.

Blackberry Yogurt Matzah Brei

Prep time: 40 minutes • inactive prep time: 1 hour • Cook time: 10 minutes • Makes: 2 servings

Matzah brei is matzah fried with eggs; it creates a blank canvas for sweet or savory toppings. With a blackberry sauce, sage and this version has a little of each.

For candied sage

¼ cup (60 ml) water

½ cup (100 g) granulated sugar, plus
    more for sprinkling

20 fresh sage leaves

For sauce

1 cup (145 g) blackberries, plus more
    for garnish

¼ cup (50 g) granulated sugar

2 tablespoons dry red wine (or water
    or Manischewitz)

¼ cup (60 ml) water

1 teaspoon orange or lemon zest
    (I use orange)

For whipped yogurt

½ cup (115 g) full-fat Greek yogurt
    (plain or a flavor works too)

¼ cup (60 ml) heavy whipping cream

¼ cup (28 g) powdered sugar

For matzah brei

2 pieces (56 g) matzah, broken into
    bite-sized pieces

Warm water

3 eggs, whisked

½ teaspoon ground cinnamon

¼ teaspoon vanilla

2 tablespoons light brown sugar

¼ teaspoon kosher salt

2 tablespoons unsalted butter

2 tablespoons slivered almonds
    for garnish

1. First, make the candied sage. Set aside a greased cooling rack or wax paper. In a small saucepan, bring water and sugar to a boil, then lower to a simmer, stirring frequently. Simmer until sugar is completely dissolved, about 2 minutes.

2. Remove from heat and let cool completely. Brush glaze on both sides of sage leaves and sprinkle with more sugar. Place leaves on cooling rack or wax paper for 1 hour or until hard. (The exact time will depend on factors like humidity.)

3. Then, make the blackberry syrup. Bring blackberries, sugar, wine, water, and zest to a boil in a medium saucepan over medium-high heat. Stir to dissolve sugar. Lower heat, and let simmer for 10 minutes; strain, and let cool to room temperature. Sauce will thicken as it cools.

4. Lastly, make the whipped Greek yogurt topping. Using a hand mixer, whip Greek yogurt and cream on medium speed until light and fluffy, about 2 minutes. Then add powdered sugar and beat until combined. Keep in the refrigerator until ready to use.

5. Finally, time for the matzah brei! Soak matzah pieces in a small bowl of warm water for 15 seconds and drain. In a separate bowl, whisk together eggs, cinnamon, vanilla, brown sugar, and salt and add matzah to the bowl.

6. Heat a medium nonstick sauté pan over medium heat. Add butter and melt. Once melted, add matzah mixture to the pan and sauté while gently stirring until eggs are set, about 5 minutes.

7. Divide matzah brei between 2 plates and garnish with whipped Greek yogurt, blackberry syrup, more blackberries, whipped Greek yogurt, almonds, and candied sage.

Tip

You can make the sage leaves up to two days ahead of time. Store uncovered in one layer in the refrigerator. You'll have leftover candied sage. Serve with fish, chicken, or (post-Pesach) pasta.

Rainbow Sprinkle Macaroons

Prep time: 15 minutes • Cook time: 15 minutes • Makes: 20 macaroons

Nothing could be more me than these festive rainbow sprinkle macaroons! (Plus, rainbow food has no calories. It's just science.) Canned macaroons seem to mysteriously show up at every Passover Seder, but no will ever admit to bringing them. These, on the other hand, you'll want to take credit for.

2 egg whites, at room temperature

1/3 cup (132 g) granulated sugar

1 teaspoon vanilla extract

Pinch salt

1½ cups (128 g) unsweetened large coconut flakes

1½ cups (140 g) sweetened flaked coconut

½ cup rainbow sprinkles, plus more for sprinkling

1. Preheat oven to 325°F/170°C. Line a baking sheet with parchment paper and set aside.

2. In a large bowl with a stand mixer with a whisk attachment or using a hand mixer, beat egg whites on medium-high speed to get soft peaks. You can also beat the egg whites by hand, but it will take a while.

3. Add sugar and beat until you have very thick, shiny, stiff peaks, about 4 minutes. You'll know you have stiff peaks when, after dipping your whisk into the egg whites and turning it upside down, the mixture will stick straight up and not dribble off.

4. Then gently stir in vanilla, salt, and coconut. The 2 different types of coconut add varying textures. Lastly, gently stir in sprinkles just until combined. Yay, sprinkles!

5. Drop heaping tablespoon-size dollops of batter on baking sheet. You may have to futz around with them after to make them nice and round, but don't make them too perfect! Those crispy stray pieces are delicious when browned. Sprinkle a few extra sprinkles on top.

6. Bake for about 15 minutes until the macaroons are just starting to brown and are dry to the touch. They will firm up as they cool. Do not overcook or they will be dry.

7. Cool on baking sheet for 5 minutes or until you can handle them, and then finish cooling on cooling rack.

Tip

The secret to this recipe is a mix of large unsweetened coconut and sweetened smaller pieces for a variety in taste and texture. Keep cooled macaroons in an airtight container for up to five days.

Layered Chocolate-Mint Meringue Cake
aka Pavlova

Prep time: 1 hour 30 minutes • inactive prep time: 2–2 ½ hours • cook time: 2 hours • Makes: 8–10 servings

Passover desserts just don't have the best reputation. I think the problem is trying to take traditional recipes and make them Passover friendly. I don't have chocolate cake most days of the year, so I certainly can go a week without a matzah-meal version. The key is choosing desserts that are already free of flour, like macaroons and meringues. With just egg whites and sugar as a base, meringues are about as natural as they come. Turning chocolate meringues into a layered cake (aka pavlova) just makes for a pretty presentation.

For cake
6 egg whites, at room temperature
2 cups (400 g) superfine sugar
 (process granulated sugar in a food
 processor to get superfine sugar)
2 teaspoons almond extract
3 tablespoons unsweetened cocoa
 powder
4 ounces (114 g) semisweet chocolate,
 melted and cooled

For whipped cream
2 cups (475 ml) heavy whipping cream
½ cup (60 g) whole mint leaves
8 ounces (227 g) cream cheese,
 softened
½ cup (57 g) confectioner's sugar
1 teaspoon vanilla extract

For garnish (optional)
Chocolate shavings
Mint leaves

1. Start with making the cake. Preheat oven to 225°F/110°C. Using an 8-inch (20 cm) bowl or round cake pan as a template, draw 3 circles on 2 parchment paper–lined baking sheets. The cake won't spread, so don't worry if the circles are close to each other. Flip paper over so the pen marks are on the bottom. Set aside.

2. In a large clean, dry bowl with a stand mixer or hand mixer with clean, dry beaters, beat egg whites on medium-high speed until soft peaks form. Gradually add sugar, 1 tablespoon at a time, and beat until you have stiff peaks and the sugar is dissolved (you can test this by rubbing a little of the meringue between your fingers; it shouldn't be gritty).

3. Fold in almond extract and cocoa powder until combined. Drizzle in chocolate and fold until incorporated. Don't worry if there is a little marbling; it's pretty! Don't over-mix or your meringue may fall.

4. Spoon meringue evenly onto the circles and bake for 2 hours or until very crisp to the touch. Rotate the pans halfway through baking. Once ready, turn off the oven, leave oven door open a crack (which, ironically, prevents cracks), and let the cakes cool in the oven at least 2 hours.

5. While your cakes are baking, make the mint whipped cream. Place cream and mint leaves in a small saucepan and bring to a simmer over medium heat. Remove from heat, and let steep for 30 minutes. Refrigerate cream until very cool, at least 2 hours or, ideally, overnight.

6. Once cream is cool, remove leaves. Beat cream cheese, sugar, and vanilla in a large bowl with a stand or hand mixer until light and fluffy. Slowly drizzle in cream while beating until you have stiff peaks.

7. Once cakes are cooled, carefully remove from parchment paper. If they crack a little, don't worry! You are covering these babies with whipped cream.

8. Place one cake on a plate or cake plate and top with a layer of whipped cream. Top with another cake, more whipped cream, and the third layer of cake and more whipped cream. Refrigerate cake 1 hour, and keep refrigerated until ready to serve.

9. Slice cake when cold, but bring to room temperature before serving. Garnish with chocolate shavings and more mint if desired. (Mini chocolate chips also make a fun garnish!) The whipped cream will soften the meringue to a chewy, rich, fudgy texture.

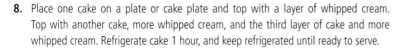

Tip

Keep your meringue cake refrigerated. It's easier to cut it cold and then bring it to room temperature to eat. Make the meringues and infuse the mint in the whipped cream the day before serving.

Manischewitz Ice Cream

Prep time: 45 minutes • Inactive prep time: 2 hours 30 minutes • Cook time: 40 minutes • Makes: 6–8 servings

Manischewitz ice cream is one of the most popular recipes on *What Jew Wanna Eat*, maybe because it seems so ludicrous it just has to be good. And it is. Here, I take it up a notch with coordinating brown butter charoset topping and salted Manischewitz caramel (see page 70 for recipes).

For ice cream

1 750-ml bottle Manischewitz, preferably blackberry (about 3 cups if using a larger bottle)
1 cinnamon stick (optional)
2 cups (480 ml) half-and-half
1 cup (235 ml) whole or 2% milk
½ cup (100 g) granulated sugar
1 teaspoon vanilla extract
6 egg yolks whisked

1. First, make the ice cream. In a medium saucepan, bring Manischewitz to a boil with the cinnamon stick if using. Reduce heat and simmer until liquid is reduced to 1 cup (235 ml), about 30–40 minutes. Cool.

2. In a large saucepan, combine half-and-half, milk, sugar, and vanilla; bring to a boil and then remove from heat. Place egg yolks in a large heatproof bowl. Temper hot liquid into the egg yolks by adding a little at a time and mixing so as to not cook the eggs. Return the whole mixture to the cream saucepan and cook over medium-low heat until the custard is thick enough to coat the back of a spoon (run your finger down the center of the coated spoon; it should leave a trail), about 10 minutes. Make sure not to let the mixture boil or it will curdle.

3. Strain the custard through a strainer into a bowl and stir in the reduced Manischewitz (removing the cinnamon stick first).

4. Cover and freeze for 30 minutes or until chilled. Then freeze in your ice cream maker according to the manufacturer's directions usually, at least 2 hours until ready to serve.

Pro Move

Serve leftover ice cream betwixt two black and pink cookies post-Passover!

Tip

I recommend the blackberry variety of Manischewitz for the best flavor, and the large 1.5-liter size if making all three components. Manischewitz caramel will keep in the refrigerator, covered, for about one week, if it lasts that long. Bring to room temperature before serving. Charoset will last up to five days; serve warm. If you don't have an ice cream maker, the charoset and caramel are awesome over store-bought vanilla too!

Brown Butter Charoset and Salted Manischewitz Caramel

Prep time: 15 minutes • Cook time: 15 minutess

Why use precious Manischewitz in just one dessert element when you can use it in three?

For brown butter charoset topping

2 tablespoons unsalted butter

¼ cup dark or light brown sugar

¼ cup (40 g) chopped walnuts, plus extra for garnish

2 Granny Smith apples (about 1½ pounds/680 g), peeled, cored, and diced into ¼–½ inch (6–10 mm) pieces

1 teaspoon ground cinnamon

¼ teaspoon vanilla extract

¼ teaspoon kosher salt

¼ teaspoon black pepper

2 tablespoons Manischewitz (blackberry preferred)

1½ teaspoons lemon juice (from ½ lemon)

For salted Manischewitz caramel

1 cup (235 ml) Manischewitz (blackberry preferred)

1 cup (100 g) granulated sugar

¼ cup (60 ml) heavy whipping cream

1 teaspoon salt

1. To make brown butter charoset topping, heat a medium sauté pan over medium-low heat and add butter. Stir until butter turns golden brown, being careful not to burn, about 2 minutes.

2. Then add the brown sugar, walnuts, and apples; stir to coat the apples and walnuts in melted sugar, about 2 minutes. Add cinnamon, vanilla, salt, pepper, Manischewitz, and lemon juice. Sauté until apples are tender but not mushy and liquid thickens and reduces, about 5 minutes. Keep warm.

3. To make Manischewitz caramel, combine Manischewitz and sugar in a medium saucepan or deep sauté pan. Bring to a boil, and then reduce heat to a simmer. Simmer until the liquid reduces by about half and starts to thicken, about 15 minutes. Remove from heat and add cream and salt. Stir to combine. The caramel will still be runny but thicken as it cools. If it is still runny once cool, simmer again to reduce further. Serve at room temperature.

4. Serve Manishcewitz ice cream with brown butter charoset topping, salted Manischewitz caramel, whipped cream (if desired), and more walnuts.

Latkes, Egg Creams, Kugel, and More!

My Bubbe is big into freezer food. As soon as we would arrive for a visit in her Boston-area home, out would come the tin foil. There were cakes, cookies, bagels, even entire roasts. A regular clown car of Jewish food, considering her freezer was no bigger than the average. I try to eat as much fresh food as possible, but sometimes it's nice to have a little something extra on hand for guests, or kindelah (children).

Chocolate-Lime Sufganiyot

Prep time: 1 hour • Inactive prep time: 2 hours 30 minutes • Cook time: 15 minutes • Makes: about 15 doughnuts

I first started to see food on another level when I studied abroad in Barcelona my senior year of college. Now this may have been the sangria talking, but the best thing I discovered was warm churros, fried and dipped in a chocolate sauce. Their version had a hint of lime, and was my inspiration for these Hanukkah doughnuts. We eat fried foods on Hanukkah to commemorate how a little oil burned for eight full days when the Maccabees rededicated the Second Temple after their victory over the Syrian-Greeks.

For dough

2¼ teaspoons (1 packet) active dry yeast

²/₃ cup (155 ml) warm whole milk (110°F/43°C)

½ cup (100 g) plus 2 teaspoons granulated sugar, divided

3¼–4 cups (460–570 g) all-purpose flour, plus more for rolling dough

2 teaspoons lime zest (from 2 medium limes)

2 tablespoons lime juice (tip: warm limes slightly in microwave to get more juice out)

2 eggs, at room temperature

1 teaspoon kosher salt

½ stick or ¼ cup (55g) unsalted butter, at room temperature

4 cups (950 ml) oil for frying, plus more as needed (use an oil with a high smoke point such as canola, grape seed or vegetable oil)

1. Combine yeast, warm milk, and 2 teaspoons sugar in a large bowl of a stand mixer and stir to dissolve. Wait 10 minutes, the mixture should get foamy. If it doesn't the milk was probably too hot, too cold, or the yeast is dead. Try again!

2. To the yeast mixture, add 3¼ cups (460 g) flour and remaining sugar and stir to combine. Then add lime zest, and juice and stir to combine. Add eggs, one at a time, and mix with the dough hook until dough starts to come together. Then add salt and combine.

3. With the mixer on low, add butter, a little at a time, until it's incorporated into the dough. Then, mix on medium speed for about 5–10 minutes until dough is completely smooth and shiny. Make sure to scrape down the sides as you mix so everything gets incorporated.

4. Knead dough on a floured surface until slightly tacky but no longer sticky, adding more flour if needed, about 5 minutes.

5. Coat a large bowl with oil and place dough inside. Let rise in a warm place until doubled in size, about 2 hours.

6. Meanwhile, make the chocolate-lime filling. Place egg yolks in a medium bowl and set aside.

7. In a medium saucepan, whisk together sugar, cornstarch, cocoa powder, and salt. Then stir in milk. Heat over medium-low heat while stirring until thick, about 10 minutes. It takes a little while, so be patient!

8. Remove from heat and whisk until you have a thick, smooth, pudding-like consistency. Then add chocolate, butter, and lime zest and stir until smooth.

9. Add chocolate mixture to the eggs a little at a time so not to cook the raw eggs. Then put the mixture in the original saucepan and heat over medium-low heat just until warm to incorporate eggs. Strain if there are any little cooked egg pieces. Let cool and transfer to a pastry or plastic bag with a round tip. Refrigerate for 2 hours.

10. When the dough is ready, punch it down and transfer to a lightly floured surface. Roll dough out to ¾-inch (2 cm) thick and cut out doughnuts using a 3-inch (7.5 cm) round cutter. Roll out scraps to make more doughnuts. Place doughnuts on parchment paper–lined baking sheets about 1 inch (2.5 cm) apart. Cover loosely with plastic wrap and let rise in a warm place until they puff up, about 1 hour. At this point, you can refrigerate them for up to 2 hours if you're not ready to fry them. Bring to room temperature before frying.

For filling

4 egg yolks, at room temperature

1/3 cup (132 g) granulated sugar

2 tablespoons cornstarch

2 tablespoons cocoa powder

1/4 teaspoon kosher salt

1 cup (235 ml) whole milk

4 ounces (113 g) semisweet chocolate chips or chopped chocolate bars

2 tablespoons unsalted butter

1 teaspoon lime zest (from 1 lime)

Powdered sugar for garnish

11. When ready to fry, heat 2 inches (5 cm) of oil in a heavy-bottomed pot until it reaches 350°F/180°C. Working in batches and being careful not to overcrowd the pan, fry the doughnuts. Flip them halfway through until both sides are golden brown, about 1–2 minutes per side. Let cool on cooling rack.

12. When doughnuts are cool enough to touch, poke a hole in the top using the tip of the pastry bag. Fill with chocolate-lime filling until doughnut has some heft to it and garnish with powdered sugar. Eat!

Tip

Doughnuts require deep-frying. Don't freak out! Invest in a deep-fry thermometer to keep track of the temperature and make sure your oil isn't getting too hot. Keep your frying station clean and dry—you don't want any rogue kitchen tools or ingredients falling in the oil.

Dessert Latkes with Fruit Compote and Marshmallow Sour Cream

Prep time: 1 hour • Inactive prep time: 35 minutes • Cook time: 45 minutes • Makes: 15 latkes

Hanukkah is all about the fried food. Luckily, the holiday occurs smack in the middle of winter, when a little more cushioning around the waist is welcome. These latkes are a testament to that. Latkes are fried grated potato cakes, sort of a Jewish hash brown. They are typically savory, but I created a sweet version with a super-simple marshmallow sour cream sauce, and a pear and cranberry compote instead of the traditional applesauce. I like sprinkling the sweet topping on post-fry so you can have a few plain latkes if you like. Plus, it keeps them extra crispy, which is exactly what we want.

For marshmallow sour cream

1¼ cups marshmallow crème
½ cup (115 g) sour cream

For compote

1 tablespoon unsalted butter
1 pear, peeled, cored, and diced
  (Bartlett or Anjou work great),
  about 1 cup (150 g)
2 cups (220 g) fresh or thawed frozen
  cranberries
¼ cup (60 ml) wine (sweet or dry, red
  or white works great; use what you
  have open!)
½ cup (115 g) light or dark brown
  sugar, or more if you want a
  sweeter sauce
1 teaspoon ground cinnamon
½ teaspoon nutmeg
¼ teaspoon ground ginger

1. To make marshmallow sauce, whisk together marshmallow crème and sour cream until smooth. Refrigerate until ready to use.

2. To make pear-cranberry compote, melt butter in a large saucepan over medium heat. Then add pears and sauté for 2–3 minutes until they start to soften. Add remaining ingredients, and simmer until cranberries pop and the mixture is thick, about 10–15 minutes. Cover to keep warm.

3. In a separate small bowl, whisk together brown sugar, cinnamon, nutmeg, cayenne, and ½ teaspoon salt for the latke topping. Set aside.

4. To make latkes, have a cooling rack nearby. Shred potatoes using the large holes of a hand grater into a bowl of ice water and let sit for 10 minutes.

5. Remove the potatoes (you may need gloves since the water is very cold) and squeeze out any extra moisture (as much as possible) into the water bowl. Finish drying potatoes really, really well with a towel.

6. Let water sit for 15 minutes to allow the starch to build up on the bottom of the bowl. Carefully drain water and reserve the milky white starch. You may have to scrape it off with a spoon. Dry the bowl very well.

7. Return shredded potatoes to the large bowl. Then add in egg, reserved starch, flour or matzah meal, and salt and stir to combine.

8. Heat a ¼-inch (6 mm) layer of oil in a large sauté pan over medium heat. You'll know the oil is ready if a small bit of latke batter sizzles when placed in oil. (You may have to add more oil as you fry; make sure to wait for it to heat back up.) Scoop ¼-cup dollops of the latke mixture into oil and flatten slightly; fry until golden brown, about 2–3 minutes. Flip and fry on the other side. If your latkes aren't holding together, try to add a little more flour and egg.

9. Drain briefly on paper towels and place on cooling racks. Sprinkle with sugar mixture, and serve immediately with compote, marshmallow sour cream, and pecans. If not eating immediately, cover lightly with foil to keep warm or keep warm in a 200°F/93°C oven.

For latkes

¾ cup (170 g) dark brown sugar

2 teaspoons ground cinnamon

¼ teaspoon ground nutmeg

Pinch cayenne

1½ teaspoons kosher salt, divided

2 pounds (900 g) russet potatoes, washed and peeled

1 egg

¼ cup (36 g) all-purpose flour or matzah meal

½ cup (120 ml) neutral high burning point oil

¼ cup pecans (25 g), for garnish

Tip

Grate your potatoes by hand! Unless you are making latkes for hundreds, it's only a few potatoes and the texture is superior. For crispy latkes, and get your potatoes as dry as possible. Make sure the oil is hot—latkes should sizzle but not brown immediately. Hot oil is key for latkes that hold together and crisp up. Don't crowd the pan! Too many latkes cool down the oil. And please don't use a nonstick pan. We want caramelized, golden brown latkes!

Peach and Goat Cheese Noodle Kugel

Prep time: 40 minutes • Cook time: 1 hour 10 minutes • Makes: 12–16 servings

This version of the noodle casserole is laced with sweet peaches and covered in an addicting goat cheese and brown sugar topping—it also freezes like a dream. And trust me, you will dream of this kugel. Here's a fact for you: Kugel used to be savory. It was our American ancestors that added the canned fruit and cornflake toppings. Sweet noodle kugel makes an excellent side dish or breakfast.

For noodles

6 tablespoons unsalted butter, plus
   more for greasing pan
1 pound (455 g) wide egg noodles
4 large firm peaches (about 5 cups/1
   kg) peeled and diced
¾ cup (150 g) granulated sugar,
   divided
1 cup (235 ml) whole milk
4 eggs, at room temperature, whisked
1½ teaspoons vanilla extract
1 teaspoon lemon zest (from 1 lemon)
1 teaspoon kosher salt
¼ teaspoon fresh cracked black
   pepper
8 ounces (227 g) full-fat sour cream
16 ounces (453 g) full-fat cottage
   cheese

For topping

1 stick or ½ cup (112 g) unsalted
   butter, melted and cooled
¾ cup (61 g) rolled oats
¾ cup (170 g) light or dark brown
   sugar
¾ cup (94 g) slivered or chopped
   almonds, plus ¼ cup (31 g) garnish
½ pound (227 g) goat cheese,
   softened

1. Preheat oven to 350°F/180°C. Then butter a deep 13 x 9-inch (33 x 23 cm) glass or ceramic baking dish and set aside.

2. Cook noodles in a large stockpot of salted water according to package directions until al dente.

3. While noodles are cooking, toss peaches in ¼ cup (50 g) sugar (or use 5 cups of canned peaches). Set aside.

4. Drain cooked noodles well, then return the noodles to the pot, add butter and gently mix, completely coating the noodles. Admire the delicious simplicity of buttered noodles.

5. In a large bowl, whisk together milk, eggs, remaining ½ cup (100 g) sugar, vanilla, lemon zest, salt, and pepper. Then gently mix in sour cream and cottage cheese.

6. Combine the dairy mixture with the noodles. Then mix in peaches just until combined.

7. To make topping, mix together all ingredients in a medium bowl with your (clean!) hands or a spoon until combined.

8. Transfer noodle mixture to the baking dish and top evenly with topping. Bake for 50–60 minutes or until golden brown and cooked through. If the top starts to get too brown, cover with foil.

9. Garnish with more almonds and serve warm or at room temperature.

Tip

Kugel freezes well for up to three months. Serve at room temperature, or reheat covered in a 250°F/120°C oven until warm. Remove covering for last few minutes to crisp up the topping.

Fon-"Jew" Manischewitz Chocolate Fondue

Prep time: 10 minutes • Cook time: 10 minutes • Makes: 12 servings

Get it? Like fondue for Jews? Fon-"Jew"! I know; it's just too good. Try not to lick the book.

½ cup (120 ml) heavy cream
12 ounces (340 g) semisweet
   chocolate
½ cup (120 ml) Manischewitz wine
   (I like blackberry)
Pinch cayenne pepper (optional)
Marshmallows, rugelach, fruit,
   matzah pieces, babka, mini pink
   and whites, challah pieces, and/
   or mandel bread pieces, for
   serving

1. In a large saucepan, bring cream to a simmer over medium heat. Then add chocolate, and reduce heat to medium-low. Stir to melt the chocolate. Then stir in the wine and cayenne, if using, until smooth and thick.

2. Serve in a fondue pot or, if you don't have one, fondue will keep warm in a bowl for 20 minutes. Place your favorite dippers on the side.

Tip
How fun and retro is it to have fondue at a party? I'm obsessed. Get all meshugenah (crazy) with your dippers! I highly suggest cubes of babka.

Strawberry-Almond Egg Cream

Prep time: 15 minutes • Cook time: 15 minutes • Makes: 2 servings

Here's something confusing: Egg cream does not contain eggs or cream. There are some conflicting rumors regarding the origin of the strangely named fountain drink from Brooklyn. Some say it did once have eggs and cream in it, but the ingredients were costly, so they changed it up. Others think the white foamy top resembles whipped egg whites. And still others think egg cream is just a mispronunciation of the drink's Yiddish name. (If you've ever heard someone speak Yiddish, this is a distinct possibility.) Regardless, I'm glad this unique drink exists. While U-Bet Chocolate Syrup is traditional, I made a strawberry syrup.

For strawberry syrup

½ cup (120 ml) water

1 cup (200 g) granulated sugar

2 cups (340 g) strawberries, hulled and quartered, about 1 pint

For egg cream

6 tablespoons strawberry syrup (plus more if you like it sweeter)

½ teaspoon almond extract, divided

2 cups (475 ml) cold milk (I use whole, but 2% works great)

²/₃ cup (155 ml) chilled seltzer (even better from a siphon bottle)

1. To make strawberry syrup, combine water and sugar in a large saucepan over medium-high heat until sugar dissolves.

2. Then add strawberries, reduce heat to medium, and simmer for 7–8 minutes, stirring periodically, until berries are very mushy. Strain strawberries, then put liquid in a bowl to cool. (Do not push down on strawberries while straining.) Let cool and refrigerate. Save the strawberries for something fun like a topping for waffles. Syrup keeps for up to 2 weeks refrigerated.

3. When ready to make the egg cream, pour 3 tablespoons cooled strawberry syrup, or more if you like it sweeter, into the bottom of 2 glasses. (You'll have some syrup leftover.) Add ¼ teaspoon almond extract and 1 cup (235 ml) milk to each glass and stir to blend. Add the seltzer and serve immediately!

Tip

If you have a siphon bottle for the seltzer, this makes the drink taste extra authentic. Use the leftover syrup with vodka or ice cream! Or vodka and ice cream!

Lemon-Lavender Blintzes

Prep time: 1 hour • Inactive prep time: 2 hours 30 minutes–12 hours • Cook time: 45 minutes • Makes: 7–8 blintzes

I have a lot of fond memories of baking blintzes with my Bubbe. Great for Shavuot, when we eat all the dairy, this recipe is also fun for the not-as-popular holiday of Tu B'Shvat which celebrates the importance of trees.

For lavender cream

1 cup (235 ml) heavy whipping cream
2 teaspoons dried food-grade lavender
2 cups (460 g) Greek yogurt
½ cup (57 g) powdered sugar (plus more if you like sweeter cream)

For batter

1 cup (142 g) all-purpose flour
1 tablespoon granulated sugar
¼ teaspoon kosher salt
3 eggs, at room temperature, whisked
1 cup (235 ml) whole milk, at room temperature
1 teaspoon vanilla extract
1 tablespoon unsalted butter, melted and cooled, plus more for cooking

For filling

4 ounces (115 g) cream cheese, at room temperature
1 cup (250 g) full-fat ricotta
¼ cup (60 g) plain Greek yogurt
½ cup (57 g) powdered sugar, plus more for garnish
1 egg
2 teaspoons lemon zest (from 2 lemons)
⅛ teaspoon kosher salt

For garnish

½ cup (57 g) powdered sugar
Optional fresh diced fruit and almonds

1. Start by preparing the lavender cream. Bring cream and lavender to a simmer in a small saucepan over medium heat. Remove from heat and let sit, covered, for 30 minutes to intensify lavender flavor. Strain out lavender and refrigerate cream to chill, covered, at least 2 hours or up to overnight. Then whip infused cream with a whisk or hand mixer until you have medium peaks. Add yogurt and powdered sugar and continue whipping until thick.

2. To make the blintz batter, combine flour, sugar, and salt in a large bowl. Add eggs, and whisk to combine, then add milk, vanilla, and butter and whisk by hand or with an electric mixer until no lumps remain. It should be the consistency of a slightly runny pancake batter. Let batter rest in refrigerator, covered, at least 1 hour or up to 2 days.

3. While batter is chilling, make filling by blending together cream cheese, ricotta, Greek yogurt, powdered sugar, egg, lemon zest, and salt with an electric mixer just until combined. Refrigerate until ready to use to help it firm up.

4. Now, time to assemble! Set aside 4 sheets of parchment or wax paper (each one big enough to fit two 9-inch [23 cm] blintz pancakes side by side). To make blintzes, butter a 9-inch (23 cm) nonstick pan with a thin coat of butter over medium heat. Then pour ⅓ cup (80 ml) of batter into the pan. Swirl pan to coat evenly. After about a minute you will see the edges begin to curl up and the blintz be will dry to the touch—it's done! Do not flip. Slide blintzes, with the help of a spatula, onto parchment or wax paper to cool. Do not layer blintzes or they will stick. Repeat with remaining batter, buttering the pan after each one. You can keep cooked blintzes in the refrigerator for up to 2 days, layered between sheets of wax paper. Or freeze for up to 2 months.

5. Spread 2–3 tablespoons of cheese mixture toward bottom of each blintz on the cooked side. Fold bottom of blintz up to cover filling and then fold the sides in. Roll like a little Jewish burrito. Assembled blintzes can be wrapped well and frozen for up to 2 months.

6. Add 1 tablespoon butter to medium nonstick pan over medium-high heat and cook on each side until golden brown, or about 1–2 minutes per side. Top warm blintzes with lavender cream, fruit, powdered sugar and almonds, if using.

Tip

Find dried lavender with dried bulk tea or herbs. The batter recipe can be used with any of your favorite fillings. Get crafty! Assembled blintzes can be wrapped well and frozen for up to two months. Once you fry them, eat right away

Pistachio-Chocolate Krembos

Prep time: 1 hour 30 minutes • Inactive prep time: 3 hours • Cook time: 40 minutes • Makes: About 18–20 cookies

What in the name of Elijah is a krembo, you may be asking. This chocolate-dipped marshmallow cookie magic is seen as a winter alternative to ice cream in Israel. I took mine up a notch with homemade pistachio cookies and marshmallow filling.

For pistachio cookie base

1½ cups (213 g) all-purpose flour
½ cup (57 g) powdered sugar
½ teaspoon kosher salt
1½ sticks or ¾ cup (140 g) chilled
    unsalted butter, cut into chunks
½ cup (150 g) unsalted, shelled
    pistachios, plus more chopped
    for garnish
1 egg
½ teaspoon vanilla extract

For marshmallow filling

6 egg whites
1½ cups (300 g) granulated sugar
½ teaspoon cream of tartar
1½ teaspoons vanilla extract

For chocolate shell

1 package (12 ounce/340 g)
    semisweet chocolate chips
3 tablespoons coconut oil, butter,
    or canola oil (I like coconut oil
    best, but use what you have)

1. To make cookies, place flour, powdered sugar, and salt in a food processer and pulse until combined. Then add butter, pistachios, egg, and vanilla. Pulse until pistachios are very fine and dough comes together. Form a log about 2 inches (5 cm) in diameter on wax paper, using the wax paper to help you mold it. Wrap in plastic wrap and refrigerate until firm, about 2 hours. If you are in a rush, freeze for 30 minutes.

2. Preheat oven to 350°F/180°C. Cut log into ¼-inch (6 mm) slices, and bake on a parchment paper–lined baking sheet, 1 inch (2.5 cm) apart, until lightly golden, about 15 minutes. Cool.

3. While cookies are baking, make your filling. Make sure the bowl and whisk are very clean and dry. Make a double boiler with a pot or heatproof bowl set over a pot of simmering water (not touching the water) and place egg whites, sugar, and cream of tartar in the top pot over simmering water over medium heat. Whisk for 5 minutes, or until sugar has dissolved. Do not let it boil. Mixture should be frothy, warm, and not gritty. If you have a candy thermometer, it should be about 140°F/60°C. Remove from heat, transfer to a large heat-resistant bowl (or use the bowl it's already in) and beat with a stand or hand mixer with whisk attachment until thick, shiny, and stiff peaks form, 10 minutes or more. Then beat in vanilla.

4. To make krembos, put filling in a pastry bag with a wide tip or a plastic bag with wide tip. Pipe onto cookies in a swirl, about 2 inches (5 cm) high, and freeze for at least 1 hour.

5. Meanwhile, to make chocolate coating, melt chocolate and oil over medium heat in a double boiler until chocolate is melted and shiny.

6. Dip chilled krembos in the chocolate (or just get messy and pour it on top) and sprinkle with extra pistachios. The chocolate should harden right away; refrigerate if not eating right away.

Tip

Cookie dough can be made up to four days ahead. Baked cookies can be stored in an airtight container at room temperature up to three days ahead.

Index

Acknowledgments

This cookbook wouldn't exist without my parents, Laurie and Lester, who are always kvelling and never questioned when I quit my responsible adult job to go to culinary school. Or my brother, Andrew, who encouraged me to "do Jew food" when I had the idea to start a blog, and always pushes me to take it to the next level—I could not be more proud to have him as a friend. Or my Bubbe, who I think is the greatest thing since sliced challah; I hope she thinks the same of me.

Thanks to Nicole, who let me destroy her kitchen for months while testing and photographing recipes and didn't mind my constant barrage of sweet treats. She has been a great friend since my cupcake party days. And to Missy, who taste tested and approved nearly every recipe. And to Mindy, my Jew-food expert, who shares her wacky hybrid recipe ideas with me and took me on a Jewish food schlep of L.A. that I'll always remember. Thanks to Devin for keeping Austin extra weird with me.

Thanks to Rage Kindelsperger, editorial director at Quarto Publishing Group, who believed in the concept of my blog and let me take my creativity and run with it.

Thanks to Tim Kyle, my headshot photographer, who I met by chance but totally gets my vision of rainbows and sprinkles. And to Jessica Casarez and Billy Mercer, my hair and makeup artists extraordinaire, two people who get that there is no such thing as too much hairspray or mascara.

And thanks to my super recipe tester, Marsha Peneer Johnston, I appreciate all your suggestions and am glad I found a new friend in this cookbook-making process. And a special thanks to all my recipe testers: your enthusiastic responses, detailed feedback, and ideas helped to shape this cookbook. Tara Dupre, Audrey Timkovich, Shoshana Turin, Tracy Done, Helen Auch, Sacha Dwyer, Lisa Marcus, Kristina Wolter, Deborah Weinstein, Natahlie Halcrow, Sue Rinsky, Alex Evans, Karen Brack, Natasha Tompakov, Kate Schubert, Kate Belza, Liza Galin Asher, Dea Southward-Poirier, Lori Sandell, Jodi Barasky, Nikki Sunderland, Leora Kimmel Greene, Patti Ducoff Albert, Samantha Ferraro, Rona M. Sandler, Fran Highbloom, Barbara Appell, Andi Cohen, Jaime Richards, Cindy Kalish, Rusty "Sarah" Holmgren, Robin Katz, Marsha K. Boswell, Anabel Wood, Sue Valencia, Ann Benator, Mandi Warner, Anita Koncz, Christa MacDonald, Teresa Reichek, Patricia Campbell, Laura Daniels, Lesley Booth, Jenny Scheldberg, Evan Caplan, Shane Cusumano, Meg Fisher, Wendy Shugarman, Zehorit Heilicher, Michelle Moss, Shira Friedman, Emily Budd, Linda Isenson, Beth Dochinger, David Williams, Sue Sternberg, Pamela Berman, Jo-Ann Newman, Sherri Leibowitz, Amanda Bronson, Jamie Banaag, Kelli Mullins, Karen Babcock, Ruth Warburg, Renée Johnson, Tina Moses, Barbara Bresler, and Ilene Spector.

Resources

Some facts from *The Encyclopedia of Jewish Food*
by Gil Marks

CHOCOLATE LIME SUFGANIYOT
adapted from *Bon Appetit*

CHOCOLATE MINT MERINGUE CAKE
adapted from *Food & Wine*

CHOCOLATE OMBRÉ SEVEN LAYER RAINBOW COOKIES
adapted from *Gourmet*

CHOCOLATE PEANUT BUTTER SEA SALT BABKA
adapted from *Jerusalem: A Cookbook*
by Yotam Ottolenghi and Sami Tamimi

HONEY POMEGRANATE WHISKEY CAKE
adapted from Marcy Goldman's
Majestic and Moist New Year's Honey Cake